The British Bus Herita

CW00556306

LOCAL TRANSPORT

in

ST. HELENS

1879-1974

by

T. B. MAUND FCIT

&

M. J. ASHTON

Venture *publications*

© Venture Publications Ltd January 1995

ISBN 1 898432 58 9

NORTHERN MUNICIPAL TRANSPORT HISTORIES

Number 1   St. Helens

In course of preparation:

Oldham
Bolton
Preston

For details of other transport titles available from Venture Publications Ltd please send a stamped addressed envelope to PO Box 17 Glossop SK13 9FA

Front Cover Illustration

Representing many preserved St Helens vehicles is this AEC Swift with Marshall bodywork which operated in the fleet from 1972 to 1985. Now fully restored it can often be seen at rallies and also at the St Helens Museum of Transport, home of many other interesting vehicles.

Photo J. A. Senior

Typeset and produced electronically for the Publishers by
Mopok Graphics, 128, Pikes Lane, Glossop, Derbyshire
Printed and bound in Great Britain

CONTENTS

INTRODUCTION

The town of St. Helens was a product of the Industrial Revolution. Lying near the western edge of the Lancashire coalfield, it became the terminus of the first modern canal, which linked the town with the Mersey and facilitated a brisk trade with the salt region of Cheshire. This, in turn, brought chemical industries to the town and glassworks, breweries and the manufacture of pharmaceutical products followed. The Liverpool and Manchester Railway, the first genuine inter-city line in Britain, opened in 1830, passed to the south of the town but the St. Helens and Runcorn Gap railway, opened in 1833, crossed it at what became known as St. Helens Junction, continuing on to Widnes and, ultimately, Garston and Liverpool.

Prescot, situated on the road to Liverpool, was an ancient place of great importance in ecclesiastical and legal affairs until eclipsed by the growth of St. Helens, formed by the amalgamation of the townships of Windle, Eccleston, Sutton and Parr. Improvement Commissioners were appointed in 1845 and the town was incorporated in 1868, by which time the population had risen to 45,000; county borough status was achieved in 1889.

The population was scattered but grouped in small communities near to places of work and the need for local transport arose only in the last quarter of the 19th century. The town was served at various times by horse omnibuses, horse trams, steam trams, company-owned electric trams, municipal electric trams, trolleybuses and motor buses. The latter have run in the town continuously since 1914 though the Corporation did not itself own any until 1923. However, unlike most municipal bus systems, which tended to operate only within or close to their municipal boundaries, the powers given by Parliament to St. Helens facilitated an unusual degree of ubiquity. The town's buses could eventually be regularly seen in Liverpool, Widnes, Warrington, Wigan, Ormskirk and Southport and on special occasions in Leigh. Licences were also held for a service to Manchester but others exercised this right on the Corporation's behalf. Its activities were more like those of a company than a municipal operator.

In 1974, the Merseyside County Council was formed and a new, much enlarged Metropolitan Borough of St. Helens surrendered its buses to the Merseyside Passenger Transport Executive thus bringing to an end the story of a resourceful and individualistic municipal enterprise.

The deregulation and privatisation provisions of the Transport Act, 1985 have caused such radical changes in urban bus operation that it is necessary to explain the concepts of areas of influence which governed relations between the various operators in the past. In South Lancashire, there was a connected network of tramways stretching from Liverpool Pier Head to the Pennine foothills and the ownership of the various sections of track clearly determined the rights of the operators. This passed down to the bus operators which succeeded them and the principles were extended to other routes which had never carried tramways. Until 1930, local councils were the licensing authorities for buses and, in appropriate cases, tended to protect their own undertakings. When area Traffic Commissioners took over licensing in 1931, they perpetuated these principles, protecting established operators from competition within their areas so long as they provided adequate services, taking the good with the bad. Co-operation between adjoining operators was well established in Lancashire from tramway days, joint services across boundaries being relatively commonplace. However, these arrangements lacked flexibility and sometimes put the operators' interests before those of the travelling public.

Today, there are many who would argue that the old arrangements were superior to the current scene with its kaleidoscope of different bus liveries and constant changes to the route networks.

ACKNOWLEDGEMENTS

The authors acknowledge with gratitude the assistance of the following:-

Staff of the St. Helens Local History Library and Archive, Lancashire Record Office, Liverpool Record Office, Merseyside Passenger Transport Executive, Merseyside Record Office, Tramway Museum Society, University of Reading Rural History Centre, Public Record Office, Members of the Omnibus Society, and the PSV Circle.

Messrs. D. J. Bubier, J. E. Dunabin, S. Gilchrist, J. C. Gillham, C. W. Heaps, W. M. Little, R. Marshall, A. W. Mills, J. G. E. Nye, A. R. Phillips, and G. W. Robb.

St. Helens Tramways by the late E.K. Stretch, published by St. Helens Corporation in typescript in 1968, has been an invaluable source document. Mr Stretch intended to produce a revised version and his notes were kindly made available by the Tramway Museum Society. The following sources were also consulted:-

A Merseyside Town in the Industrial Revolution - St. Helens 1750-1900 (third impression) by T. C. Barker and J. R. Harris, Frank Cass 1993.
The Trolleybuses of St. Helens by G Sandford, Reading Transport Society, c.1967
South Lancashire Tramways by E. K. Stretch , Manchester Transport Museum Society, 1972.
The Tramways of Wigan by E. K. Stretch, Manchester Transport Museum Society, 1978
St. Helens Newspaper
St. Helens Reporter
Liverpool Daily Post and Echo
Liverpool Evening Express
Bus & Coach
Modern Transport
Motor Transport
Tramway & Railway World

Minute books of Ribble Motor Services Ltd.
Minute books of Liverpool Tramways Committee
Records of St. Helens Corporation

HORSE & STEAM

A Turnpike Trust which had been established for the Liverpool-Prescot road on 26th April 1726 was extended to St. Helens on 4th June 1746 and to Haydock and Ashton-in-Makerfield on 7th April 1753. A regular daily short stage coach service between Liverpool and Prescot commenced in November 1767 but the first service from St. Helens seems to have been Chalk's coach which was running by 1794 and left the White Hart at 10.30am daily, returning from the Bull Inn, Dale Street, Liverpool at 4.0pm in winter and 5.0pm in summer. Numerous other coaches passed through the town en route to and from Liverpool and, for a time, there was a link between the railway at St. Helens and Southport by Edward Fidler's *Patent Coach*.

In 1827 a local coach, *Regulator*, financed by several local residents including Peter Greenall, the brewer, was leased by one Lawton and ran regularly between St. Helens and Liverpool until 1833 when it was sold to a successor. By this time, a horse-drawn carriage was running on the St. Helens and Runcorn Gap Railway between the town station (then located near Peasley Cross bridge) and St. Helens Junction. The railway was more interested in goods than passengers and had made no provision for people wanting to reach the trains on the Liverpool and Manchester railway. This conveyance was running by September 1832 and continued for some years.

The powerful Busby family, based in Liverpool but with a finger in many urban transport pies from Yorkshire to the Midlands, is known to have run a Liverpool-St. Helens service. The Liverpool Road and Railway Omnibus Co. Ltd., a company registered in 1860 with Busbys as the major shareholders, established stables at Prescot and, by February 1862, was running four daily trips thence to St. Helens and three between St. Helens and Liverpool. Mr J. Phythian, a member of the family who later established a travel agency in the town, ran three times to Haydock on

Saturdays and J. Young ran four times a day on weekdays between the railway station and St. Annes (approximately the corner of Knowsley Road and Dunriding Lane) charging 2d to Boundary Lane and 3d all the way. Indeed, it is surprising that the relative isolation of St. Helens from the mainstream rail network, with direct links with Wigan and Liverpool established only in 1869 and 1872 respectively, did not lead to more of this sort of thing.

Horse Tramways Approved

The passing of the Tramways Act, 1870 established a legal framework which facilitated the construction of street tramways which were introduced in Liverpool in 1869 and Manchester in 1877. Three rival schemes for St. Helens were announced in 1878, the principal objectives in every case being a service to Prescot. Two were rejected but the third, promoted by William Busby, Philip Eberle, Francis Augustus Remmington Neill, Joseph Riley and James Melling, was authorised by Parliament on 24th July 1879. The St. Helens & District Tramways Co. was formed with a capital of £70,000 in £10 shares and lines to Prescot, Dentons Green, Haydock (Rams Head) and Marshalls Cross were authorised. The plans included a number of swing bridges across the St. Helens Canal and several crossings of mineral railways. Fares not exceeding 1d per mile were stipulated with a duty to carry workmen at half that rate (minimum 1d) on at least one car on each route before 7.0am and after 6.0pm.

By March 1880 the company had raised only £10,000 capital and further delay was caused by a dispute about the method of track-laying to be adopted. The company wanted to lay wooden sleepers on a 3 in. foundation of concrete, costing an estimated £4,946 per mile, a method which had been officially approved on several systems elsewhere and was sufficiently resilient to give a smooth, quiet ride. The Corporation, however, thought it to be too light and wanted 'Gowan's system' of girder rails on iron sleepers which the company's engineer, Charles H. Beloe, said were noisy and expensive, costing £5,600 per

Horse car No. 1 was built on the Eades principle, the body swivelling on the chassis, hence there was only one staircase. The steep gradients – Croppers Hill and Eccleston Hill, necessitated the use of a 'trace-horse', an added expense.

A delightful period view in St. Helens town centre in the 1890s showing one of the six Eades cars.

Green engine No. 8 and Milnes trailer No. 6 carrying boards for the Peasley Cross-Dentons Green through service. Note the way the engine's moving parts are completely boxed in, almost to ground level, in accordance with Board of Trade regulations, and the condensing pipes on the roof, to turn the steam back into water.

mile. Eventually, a third system, 'Barker's', as used in Manchester, was adopted within the borough. A grooved T-section rail was laid on longitudinal iron sleepers, the cost being estimated at £3,700 per mile. However, outside the borough, beyond the writ of the Corporation, some sections were laid with Beloe's system of wooden sleepers.

A contractor, A. Speight, was appointed and work started at Toll Bar on 6th October 1880 and within the then borough boundary on 26th March 1881 by which time about £24,000 of capital had been raised. As the enabling Act had given only two years for the system to be finished, a further Act, extending the time limit, had to be obtained in June 1881. The Corporation complained about the contractor and the company complained about the quality of the setts; on the whole, relations between the parties were strained.

The Prescot line was passed by the Board of Trade inspector on 3rd November 1881 and opened two days later. Work then started on the Marshalls Cross line as far as Peasley Cross, a new contractor, Charles Phillips & Co. having been engaged. The cars entered the town centre via Bridge Street and left via Westfield Street but the loop through the town was reversed after a time; the journey took 35-minutes but, as the cars ran half-hourly, there was much wasteful layover time at both ends. The ruling gradient was 1 in 30 and two horses were used throughout but on the steep gradients of Croppers Hill (1 in 19) and Eccleston Hill (1 in 21) a third 'trace horse' was needed, adding to the running costs.

The Peasley Cross line ended at Sutton Road, 700 yards short of the authorised terminus at Robins Lane. A service through to Dentons Green via Shaw Street, Corporation Street and Cotham Street, returning via Church Street started in May or June 1882, the exact date not having been determined. The Haydock line, as far as Grange Road (then known as Holly Bank Road), was opened on 5th August 1882. The terminus was nearly three-quarters of a mile short of the authorised point at the Ram's Head, the line ending just before Richard Evans' level crossing. In the town, the company had wanted to terminate the Haydock cars at Shaw Street railway station but the Corporation objected on the grounds that Haydock people would not be brought into the town centre; the Town Hall was then proposed but also rejected so the cars terminated in Cotham Street, running in and out via Corporation Street.

A depot and stables were built in Hall Street. Car and

horse requirements were:-

Prescot	3 cars	38 horses
Haydock	2 cars	23 horses (3 cars Saturdays)
Dentons Green-Peasley Cross	2 cars	23 horses (3 cars Saturdays)

The Horse Car Fleet

The first cars to be bought were of the double-deck Eade's type, built by the Ashbury Railway Carriage & Iron Co. of Manchester. This patent design enabled the body to be swivelled round on the chassis without unharnessing the horses, being held in position by locking pins. This obviated the need for a staircase at both ends, simplifying the body construction and reducing the weight. There were six of these cars which cost £180 each. There were seats for about 36 passengers with a back-to-back 'knifeboard' seat on the upper deck. Two single-deck cars, seating 18 passengers and costing £120 each, were built by the Oldbury Carriage & Wagon Co., arriving early in 1882 and a third some time later. Three conventional double-ended cars, seating 16 passengers on each deck, built by the Metropolitan Railway Carriage & Wagon Co., were in service by 1883 and these 12 cars comprised the entire rolling stock until late in the 'eighties when a 'magnificent one-horse car', a single-decker, was bought from G.F. Milnes & Co. of Birkenhead.

Financial Problems

The shareholders received a dividend, paid partly out of capital, for the first half-year ending in January 1882 but after that there were no more. While the directors blamed the hilly nature of the routes for the high cost of horse power, poor management and organisation were the true causes of the company's problems. It was decided to seek parliamentary powers to use steam engines instead of horses, a course of action facilitated by the passing of the Mechanical Power on Tramways Act, 1879. An extensive system was being planned to the north of Manchester and this no doubt influenced the directors. But the town council were opposed to steam engines in the town centre and the St. Helens & District Tramways Act, 1883 authorised the use of steam traction except in Westfield Street, Bridge Street, Cotham Street and Church Street. It was proposed to build a siding off the road at the top of Westfield Street and Bridge Street where the engine would wait while the car was taken into the town by horses and a line along the west end of Corporation Street between the Town Hall and Duke Street would avoid the use of Cotham Street by the Dentons Green-Peasley Cross cars. As there was no restriction on the use of Corporation Street by steam engines, the Haydock route could be worked throughout by steam. Powers were also granted for extensions in Prescot to the railway station via High Street, Atherton Street and Aspinall Street (0.53 miles) and from Peasley Cross to St. Helens Junction (1.32 miles).

The company had no funds available to buy steam engines and their financial affairs worsened, revenue falling off alarmingly. The fare to Haydock was reduced from 4d to 3d with a view to attracting more traffic and frequent changes to fares and stage-points tended to confuse passengers. Economies led to complaints of dirty cars, unpunctuality, rudeness of staff and breakdowns caused by poor maintenance

Manufacturers of steam tram engines refused to supply them on hire-purchase. In 1886 the directors asked each

An unidentified steam tram and trailer stand on the turning loop at Dentons Green. Note the different arrangement of the condensing pipes, suggesting that this was one of the original engines, 1-6.

A group of three steam locomotives and trailers on the loop at Dentons Green. The occasion seems to have been a children's outing and one wonders how the disruption of the ordinary services to provide so many cars was justified.

shareholder to pay £1 per £10 share to raise money for the conversion but, following further losses, blamed in part on bad winter weather, the shareholders appointed a special committee which discovered many irregularities, especially drunkenness and theft of fare money by conductors and abuse of the contract system, no tickets being issued to contractors. A new Board was elected with B.A. Dromgoole, proprietor of a local newspaper, as chairman. A through service was run between Prescot and Haydock, saving one car by eliminating the excessive layover. Unfortunately, the considerable extra revenue generated by the many reforms was absorbed on essential repairs to the cars and tracks and no dividend could be paid. The debenture holders became impatient and petitioned for the company to be wound up on 5th January 1888. A Receiver, J.C. Marsh, a Liverpool solicitor, was appointed on 15th June 1888 but, on a petition of St. Helens Corporation who wanted the tram service to continue, he was forbidden by the High Court to distribute the assets and ordered to carry on the business of the company.

The Steam Tramways

On 20th March 1889 a conditional contract was drawn up for the sale of the company to a consortium led by John Waugh, a civil engineer, of Bradford, Yorks. for £39,750. In the face of local public criticism, the Corporation withdrew its objections to steam engines in the town centre streets and a new company, the St. Helens & District Tramways Co. Limited with a capital of £50,000 was formed on 22nd October 1889. The old statutory company was never dissolved and may still, in law, exist. Six engines (1-6) were ordered from Thomas Green & Son Ltd. of Leeds and seven cars from G.F. Milnes & Co. of Birkenhead; three more cars were added later. As the

service required six engines, a seventh identical unit was ordered in May 1890 and an eighth in 1891. In accordance with the law, the engines were boxed in to within an inch or two of the ground and the steam was condensed by pipes mounted on the roof. The trailer cars were covered-top double deckers, seating 64, with outside staircases. Coloured lights were displayed at night, red for Prescot, blue for Haydock and green for Dentons Green and Peasley Cross.

Numerous improvements were made to the track, curves being eased for the larger cars and a loop constructed at Dentons Green. However, at the first inspection on 25th February 1890, the Inspecting Officer, Maj.-Gen. Hutchinson refused to pass the lines, insisting on the installation of a reversing triangle at Prescot and the repositioning of the track in Bridge Street. The wooden canal swing bridges at Redgate and Blackbrook were deemed to be inadequate for the heavier steam cars. All the lines except Haydock were passed on 3rd April and steam tram services began the following day. It can only be assumed that the company decided to run to Blackbrook (Ship Inn) illegally as steam cars were running there later in the month with a horse car beyond. Steam trams reached Haydock Cottage Hospital by August and a reversing triangle was installed at Holly Bank in September 1893 but the Redgate bridge, after reconstruction, was not passed by Maj.-Gen. Hutchinson until 5th October 1893.

It was found impossible to maintain a half-hourly service with two cars on each route and the frequency was reduced to 40-minutes, cars running from 8.0am to 10.0pm with a 7.20am car to Prescot and 10.40pm departures on all routes on Saturdays. On Sundays, the service started about noon. The Prescot service was increased to half-hourly at weekends in the summer of 1891.

St. Helens was proud of being the sole system using only compound engines but they were badly maintained and, after the manager, A. Johnson, was dismissed, it was discovered that one of the engines had been dismantled for spares without the Board's knowledge or authority. A ninth engine was ordered so that there was a spare in the event of a breakdown. The new manager, I. F. Cuttler, introduced regular maintenance procedures and the company prospered, paying dividends of between 2°% and 5% from 1894-95. Detailed figures are not available but it is believed that about 1.5 million passengers per year were carried. The track foundations had collapsed in places under the heavy weight of the engines and relaying with girder rail started on the Prescot route in 1894, the Corporation laying the setts between the tracks at the company's expense. Extensions to the Ram's Head at Haydock, to St. Helens Junction and to Thatto Heath were considered but nothing was done as the powers for the first two had long expired.

The Corporation, by the St. Helens Corporation Act, 1893, obtained powers to purchase the tramways and to operate them if no lessee could be found. This power included the lines outside the borough though the authorities concerned could purchase them from St. Helens under certain conditions. Protracted negotiations with the company were concluded in March 1897, the track being bought for £23,000 and a lease granted to the company from 1st April 1897. The length of track, of which more than half had been relaid with girder rail was as follows:-

St. Helens County Borough	6.927 miles
Whiston Rural District	1.51
Haydock Urban District	1.535
Prescot Urban District	0.263
TOTAL	10.235

In October 1897, at a time when very few tramways had been electrified, the Corporation decided to electrify the existing system and extend it. Powers were granted by the St. Helens Corporation Act, 1898, the following extensions being authorised:-

Prescot terminus to Brook Bridge	0.55 miles
Toll Bar to Prescot via Rainhill	3.75
Branch to Rainhill station	0.11
Baldwin Street to Windle	0.925
Holly Bank to Ram's Head, Haydock	0.80
Finger Post to Parr (Horse Shoe)	1.263
Peasley Cross to St. Helens Junction	1.337
Branch to Hammond St. (manure depot)	0.40
Branch to Eccleston St. (power station)	0.175
TOTAL	9.310

Meanwhile, control of the company passed into new hands, the new directors being James B. and Jacob Atherton and F. J. Leslie. The Atherton brothers were electrical pioneers, James being managing director of British Insulated Wire Company of Prescot. They were directors of several electric supply undertakings including some in Australia. They were destined to play a key role in the spread of electric tramways in South Lancashire. In order to raise the additional capital necessary, the New St. Helens and District Tramways Co. Ltd. was registered on 4th November 1898 with a capital of £150,000 in £1 shares. The chairman was Sir J. A. Willox, a Liverpool newspaper proprietor. After much discussion, the Corporation agreed to lease the tramways undertaking to the new company for 21 years from 1st October 1898.

Unidentified locomotive with trailer car 8 on the Haydock route in the 1890s.

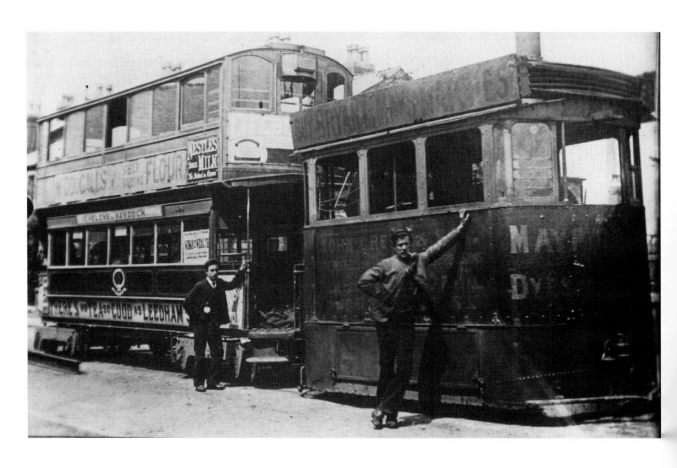

By leasing its lines to the New St. Helens & District Tramways Co. Ltd. (NStHD) the burghers of St. Helens unwittingly ensured that the electrification of the tramways ceased to become a purely local matter but rather a key event in the establishment of a tramway network stretching from the Mersey to the Pennines. The Atherton brothers were involved over the next few years in the promotion of the Lancashire Light Railways Co. Ltd. (LLR) (Prescot to Knotty Ash) and the South Lancashire Tramways Co. (SLT)(Haydock to Hindley & Atherton; Lowton to Leigh and Bolton). Other lines which were never constructed would have linked Parr with Earlestown, Newton-le-Willows and Lowton, Hindley direct to Westhoughton and Bolton, and Bolton with Darwen. Difficulty in raising capital led to the formation of an umbrella company, South Lancashire Electric Traction & Power Co. Ltd. which acquired all the shares in LLR and SLT in 1900.

Under the terms of the St. Helens lease, the NStHD was to pay rent rising from £2,400 to £3,500 per annum over 17 years and 2d per unit for electricity generated by the Corporation up to 400,000 units per annum, decreasing thereafter to 1d per unit for 800,000. The Corporation was responsible for installation and maintenance of track and electrical equipment. After inspecting a conduit car at the British Insulated Cable

works (BI), the Corporation decided upon the overhead wire system as, indeed, did almost every other tramway, the wires to be installed by BI.

The first electric cars ran in public service on 20th July 1899, to Dentons Green and Toll Bar, the full Prescot route being taken over from steam cars two days later. The frequencies were more than doubled and the electric cars rapidly gained public favour. Electric cars took over to Peasley Cross on or about 9th December 1899 and on a new route to Elephant Lane, Thatto Heath on 23rd February 1900. This was extended to the Mental Hospital (Nutgrove) on 7th April 1900, the line to Haydock (Ram's Head) opening on the same day. Steam traction then ceased though one locomotive was retained for several years.

The Parr tramway, terminating at the Horse Shoe, was opened on Whit Saturday, 2nd June 1900 and construction went ahead on the Windle and St. Helens Junction routes. Objections from the railway about the attachment of wires to the bridge in Robins Lane caused the latter to terminate at Ellamsbridge Road, 200yd short of the terminus for a few weeks after the line was

New St. Helens & District company's car 5, built by Brush in 1899, pictured when quite new. Note the very low dash-plate and the completely open platforms with no protection against the elements for the driver.

Number 2, one of the company's first bogie cars in original condition. Note the absence of destination equipment on the ends. These cars were 31ft 2in long and 6ft 10in wide and seated 67 passengers.

opened on 19th September 1900; a planned extension to the station entrance was not achieved until 1926. The short Windle route, along North Road to Hard Lane, opened on the same day.

The final sections, between Nutgrove, Rainhill, Whiston and Prescot and from Prescot to Brook Bridge on the Liverpool Road were opened in January 1901. The line along Eccleston Street to the power station was built but not connected up. This and the Hammond Street line, which was not built, were planned in connection with a scheme for burning waste matter as a cheap fuel which came to nothing. Powers were granted in 1900 for an extension from Eccleston Street to Knowsley Road (Dunriding Lane) but it was never built. Other short lines authorised at the same time were along the western end of Corporation Street and in Parr Street, designed to improve traffic flow near the town centre.

Through services

Of the original grandiose scheme, the only line authorised to the Lancashire Light Railways Co. Ltd. (LLR) was a single line tramway, 3.11 miles long, with 13 passing places, between Brook Bridge, Prescot and the Knotty Ash terminus of the Liverpool tramways. This was an essential link in the chain of tramways across South Lancashire. The line was finished by April 1902 but Liverpool Corporation was not ready so a through

quarter-hourly service between St. Helens and Knotty Ash did not begin until 24th June 1902. The links between the LLR and NStHD companies were so close that the plan to build an LLR depot at Huyton was dropped and the seven LLR cars were kept in the St. Helens shed. Eye witness accounts suggest that, after the first few years, the LLR cars worked the St.Helens-Rainhill-Prescot service while the large NStHD bogie cars ran to Knotty Ash.

On 30th March 1903, following the completion of some of the SLT lines, a convoy of six cars was driven from Liverpool Pier Head to Bolton Town Hall, via Prescot, St. Helens, Haydock, Ashton and Atherton, to demonstrate to the various civic dignitaries in the party the feasibility of through goods traffic on the tramways between Liverpool docks and the inland manufacturing towns. This, not passenger traffic, had been the Atherton brothers' vision as they realised that trams were too slow to compete with the railways for long distance passenger traffic. But there was dissatisfaction with the railways' charges for higher value goods and the trams could have offered cheaper rates. Despite optimism, nothing came of these plans as the SLT had no funds to finance the considerable track doubling which would have been necessary. The traffic was to have been carried at night in goods trailers. St. Helens council vigorously opposed the idea of goods trams passing through the town every few minutes during the night hours. Powers for goods traffic were deleted from the SLT Bill of 1903 and SLT running powers over the St. Helens lines were confined to the right to reach the LLR from Haydock; over the years there were several disputes about 'foreign' cars on the lines.

Car 34 was one of 20 cars with windscreens delivered in late 1899, seen at Nutgrove on the Rainhill route. The driver's lot was not a happy one as the Mozley reversed stairs obscured his nearside vision and the absence of a screen on the nearside created draughts. Some of these cars became trailers on the associated South Lancashire Tramways during the 1914-18 war.

A through half-hourly service between St. Helens and Liverpool Pier Head began on 18th May 1903 using LLR cars but with Liverpool Corporation crews between Knotty Ash and the Pier Head. It was not financially successful and was reduced to two trips a day in January 1904 and withdrawn altogether from 13th December 1905 though through tickets continued to be issued for some years and Liverpool cars ran through to Prescot on special occasions.

A service on the SLT line from Haydock to Hindley commenced on 4th April 1903 and continued to Atherton and Tyldesley but there was no through running to St. Helens until October 1909 when the NStHD took over operation of the Haydock-Ashton section. As there was a community of interest between Ashton and St. Helens, the through service was welcomed by the public.

Following very poor financial results, the South Lancashire Electric Traction & Power Co. went into voluntary liquidation in July 1904. A new company, Lancashire United Tramways Ltd. (LUT), was registered on 29th December 1905. The Athertons then disappeared from the scene. On 2nd January 1906, the SLETP undertaking, including the shares of LLR and SLT was sold to LUT who purchased 75% of the £5 preference shares in the New St. Helens company for £1.2.4d, (£1.11½p) per share. LUT wanted to merge both the NStHD and LLR companies with SLT but St. Helens Corporation would not agree, making it clear that it would consider the lease at an end if this was done. The new owners managed to negotiate a new lease at £1,000 less per annum, giving the St. Helens ratepayers the burden of 1d rate for tramway maintenance. The LLR was leased to the NStHD, thus formalising the existing arrangement of running the two undertakings as one.

Disputes

Company tramwaymen were generally paid lower wages than those in municipal service and St. Helens was no exception, drivers receiving £1 for an 80-hour week. Schedules were particularly tight and there were constant public complaints about accidents caused by speeding and cars failing to stop because of late running. On the Prescot service the 23-minute journey time made it quite impossible to maintain the statutory speed limit of 10 mph. Staff unrest led to a month long strike in April-May 1905 leading to the ignominious defeat of the workers and the engagement of new staff.

There were regular disagreements between the company and the Corporation, a not unfamiliar occurrence where the track and the operations were under separate control. The Corporation complained of noisy, badly maintained cars but the company said this was due to the Corporation not maintaining the track properly thus damaging the cars and claimed compensation, some of which was paid.

The 1914-18 War

The war placed a great strain on the tramways and the short Windle and Dentons Green routes were suspended for a time to release crews and cars for augmented

The car depot in Hall Street being extended in August 1899. Two steam locomotives can be seen and some electric cars already occupy the uncompleted centre section.

services on the longer routes. After the severe railway economies of 1917, the inter-connected South Lancashire tramway network provided an alternative means of making quite long journeys and local people complained of being crowded out of the Haydock and Prescot cars by people from the mill towns further inland making journeys to Liverpool. The extent of this traffic is highlighted by the increase in revenue on the Prescot-Knotty Ash line from £6,442 in 1913 to £17,695 in 1918 for a slightly lower mileage.

End of Company Operation

In 1914, the company tried and failed to get an extension of the lease which expired on 30th September 1919. There was a strong body of public opinion in favour of direct municipal ownership and this was agreed. Naturally, the company spent as little as possible on the undertaking in the last years of the lease and was able to plead wartime shortages of labour and materials. When it became certain that the lease would not be renewed, the parent company began planning for the future. The Brook Bridge-Knotty Ash line would be isolated and without a depot so it was offered to Liverpool Corporation who bought it for £18,000, taking it over on 1st October 1919. The seven cars carrying the LLR name were then transferred to SLT. In conjunction with Lancashire County Council who reconstructed the A57 road (then said to be the busiest main road outside London), Liverpool Corporation relaid much of the line as double track on a central or side reservation in 1922-23 at a cost of £132,200.

The First Bus Service

In 1914 the Corporation was concerned at the absence of transport facilities between the town and outlying areas beyond the tramway system, particularly the mining communities of Clock Face and Sutton Manor whose railway service was particularly poor. Councillor Thomas Abbott was given the task of remedying the situation and he succeeded in persuading County Carriers, a firm controlled by the Dromgoole family, to start a bus service between Sutton Manor and Market Street, St. Helens in June 1914. A separate company, St. Helens & District Motor Service Co. Ltd., was registered on 13th January 1915 with Abbott as manager and secretary and Councillor Marshall and M.C. Dromgoole among the directors. The service was an immediate success and the fleet grew rapidly. The PSV Circle claims that its eighth Hora-bodied Daimler was delivered in 1916 which suggests some wartime activities, perhaps in connection with the munitions factory in Reginald Road. In 1918, County Carriers sold its interest and the company split, Councillor Marshall forming Marshall Garages which included a substantial charabanc business.

1919-1931

St. Helens Corporation took over operation of the tramway system on 1st October 1919 amid a wave of municipal pride. Mr L.C.F. Bellamy, the son of a famous Liverpool tramways manager, was appointed as manager. Dreams of a fleet of new trams were soon dispelled when the cost was worked out and the post-war difficulties of getting them were realised. Eight cars ordered from the Brush company in July 1919 were not delivered until 1921, the quoted cost having risen through inflation from £17,500 to almost £20,000. The 36 NStHD cars were purchased by the Corporation for £24,000 and three SLT cars were hired for a time at ten shillings each per day. Essential track renewals were estimated to cost £73,000.

At Prescot, the cars now ran through the town and terminated at Brook Bridge on the western outskirts to which Liverpool's cars also ran. Prescot council agitated for a better arrangement and the section between Brook Bridge and the King's Arms was sold by St. Helens to Liverpool Corporation for £8,000 from 1st April 1921. Both Liverpool and St. Helens cars thereafter terminated at the King's Arms, where the Fusilier now stands.

St. Helens Corporation Act 1921

The Corporation now sought additional powers for its passenger transport undertaking. The St. Helens Corporation Act, 1921 granted powers to run motor buses within the borough, on specified roads outside and anywhere in extension of, or in connection with any tram, trolleybus or bus route with the approval of the local road authority and the Minister of Transport. Even on the specified routes, these approvals were necessary.

The Act also granted general powers for the operation of trolleybuses (officially termed trackless trolley vehicles). Following the passing of the Roads Act 1920, local authorities could no longer demand mileage payments from bus operators, based on the alleged wear and tear, but it was still legal to demand a sum for improving the roads up to a standard which the council thought necessary.

The Bill as drafted originally sought motor bus powers on 19 routes outside the borough. As St. Helens was the centre of a region administered by several other authorities, it was felt that a motor bus system could not prosper if it were restricted to routes within the borough boundary, especially as the tramway system penetrated into several of these districts. The Bill was opposed by the railway companies, Lancashire United Tramways Ltd. and its statutory subsidiary, South Lancashire Tramways Co., and several local authorities. The railway and LUT objections were on commercial grounds while the local authorities were concerned with wear and tear on roads. The 19 routes were reduced to eight, those eliminated including provocative routes into LUT/SLT territory, reaching as far as Lowton St. Mary's. Several rural routes in the area between Billinge, Crank and Rainford and to Knowsley village, which could scarcely have been profitable, were deleted because of the unsuitability of the roads.

The approval of Widnes Corporation was also necessary for routes in certain parts of Rainhill, Bold and other districts in which that authority held motor bus powers. The Lancashire United group was protected by clauses prohibiting competition with the tramways

Ex-company car 20 in Corporation days looks a little run down as it stands at the Horse Shoe, Parr terminus before renumbering to 32 in March 1929.

Above: Brush 4-wheel car 25, new to the Corporation in 1921 as No. 41, stands at Prescot terminus just before the end of the tramways in 1936. Liverpool Corporation car 147 arrives to stand on the remnant of the Rainhill route's track in Warrington Road. The King's Arms, for long a local landmark, has been replaced by The Fusilier.

Below: An unidentified rebuilt bogie car stands on the newly-laid curve at Ashton-in-Makerfield while working the short-lived through service between St. Helens and Wigan. Through passengers are conspicuous by their absence.

Above: Bogie car 14 was rebuilt as a covered low-height car and its bogies were replaced by a 10ft radial 4-wheel truck as shown, apparently just after completion with the proud workforce facing the camera. It was renumbered 7 in March 1929.

Below: One of two 1904 Dick Kerr bogie single deck cars bought from Wigan Corporation in 1927 is shown at St. Helens Junction terminus. Originally numbered 30-31, they became 13-14 in 1929.

South Lancashire Transport Company's bogie car 54 leaves Ashton-in-Makerfield for St. Helens about 1930; a second SLT car in the background is working the Ashton-Atherton section. There was no through running from St. Helens to Atherton in tramway days.

and on certain roads in Earlestown and Newton-le-Willows so long as LUT was providing an efficient bus service. Despite the deletions and restrictions, the powers went much further than those granted to most municipal undertakings and they enabled the Corporation to build up a very successful and extensive bus service network during the ensuing decade.

The First Motor Buses

While tram tracks were being relaid in 1921-22, the Corporation hired two buses and four drivers from the Bristol Tramways and Carriage Co. Ltd. for three months from 3rd August. They arrived early and were used on August Bank Holiday, 1st August, on routes to Billinge and Rainford. This was strictly illegal as the Act granting powers to run motor buses did not receive the Royal Assent until 4th August. Three AEC buses were also hired for short periods from Liverpool Corporation.

The local authorities at first asked for substantial payments to make the roads suitable for buses to run to Billinge and Rainford but eventually they dropped their demands as their ratepayers wanted the buses. In 1923 Ribble Motor Services Ltd., operating from a depot at Wigan, started services between St. Helens and Wigan via Billinge and St. Helens and Ormskirk via Rainford. Lancashire United also started a service to Leigh via Earlestown, a minimum fare of 4d being charged to protect the Parr trams. The Corporation hastened to start their own services and the first routes commenced on 17th August 1923 between Holme Road, Eccleston and Ormskirk Street via Knowsley Road, Cambridge Road, Horace Street, Boundary Road and Peter Street and to Washway Lane, Haresfinch via College Street. They were linked together and one bus could provide a 45-minute service. After a time, the frequency was increased to half-hourly, requiring a second bus.

The Corporation planned to start two-hourly services

to Rainford and Billinge on 22nd January 1924 but, because of a railway strike, they ran hourly to Rainford on 22-24th, starting the planned services on 25th. In September 1924, Ribble extended their Wigan-St. Helens service through to Sutton Manor and Widnes but, by 1926, this was run only on Sundays, every two hours, when the train service was very poor. From 1925, the Corporation restricted Ribble's licences and imposed minimum fares to protect their own buses and trams from competition. Similar restrictions were also placed on the St. Helens District buses which had apparently enjoyed free trade hitherto.

In November 1925, a new manager, D.E. Bell, came to St. Helens from the Yorkshire (West Riding) Tramways Co. and was destined to lay the foundations of the widespread network of later years. He recognised the strategic position of St. Helens with its unique statutory powers enabling buses to run far beyond the town's boundaries. His outlook was commercial rather than municipal and the Tramways Committee backed up his policies. A service to Burtonwood via Parr was started in January 1926 followed in March by a route to Clock Face on Mondays, Fridays and Saturdays. This established a pattern for services to the outlying mining districts many of which did not have daily services until after the 1939-45 war. In June, a Sunday service from Toll Bar to Sutton Heath and then alternately to Micklehead Green or St. Helens Junction provided a link to Taylor Park and between the southern suburbs without going through the town centre.

The first workmen's service for miners, between Finger Post and Bold Colliery, started in January 1927, others following from as far afield as Far Moor, Longshaw, Billinge and Rainford. The St. Helens & District Motor Service Co. with eight buses and a garage, was bought in June 1927 for £12,000, a sum which appears to have been excessive as, in 1931, the six remaining buses were valued at only £185 and the

This is the only known photograph of the Guy 20-seat buses which opened St. Helens Corporation's bus services in 1923-24. They are posed in the doors of the new Tolver Street garage which was opened in 1928.

garage was sold at a loss of £825. The purchase almost doubled the motor bus fleet overnight and the Sutton Manor garage had to be used for several months until a new garage in Tolver Street, behind the tram depot, was ready.

Tramway Improvements

The whole of the St. Helens Junction line was relaid during 1921-22, loops being increased and repositioned to improve timekeeping. The Prescot line was virtually doubled throughout during the 1920s and electric points installed at strategic junctions. The Junction line was extended for 110 yd to the station entrance (without powers) and a trolley reverser installed. Plans to lay track in Ormskirk Street between Sefton Place and Duke Street (again, without powers) were rejected but the tracks in the town centre were relaid in 1926. Covered double-deck cars could not pass under the low bridges at Redgate and Peasley Cross Lane and low-height cars were designed as described elsewhere. The St. Helens Junction and Dentons Green lines were separated so that the former could be run with top-covered cars.

Trolleybus Plans

The track between Prescot and Rainhill was badly worn as motor traffic on what was then one of the busiest roads in the land preferred to drive, whenever possible, in the middle of the road. The route was also one of the least profitable being quite rural in character for much of its length. This seemed to be a suitable route for trolleybuses and councillors visited a number of systems to assess their merits. In 1924, a Provisional Order was obtained for the route between Toll Bar and Prescot via Rainhill (3.78 miles) but, because of the heavy traffic through Thatto Heath, it was decided to convert only the section from Nutgrove to Prescot.

However, it was not until March 1927 that the trams were replaced temporarily by motor buses as it was found essential to reposition most of the poles, adding new ones and strengthening many of them with concrete or wire rods. The overhead equipment was installed by B.I. Cables whose works lay on the route. Rather tight turning circles were installed at each end.

Four centre-entrance single-deck trolleybuses entered service on the 2.71 mile long route on 11th July 1927, through transfer tickets being available on the trams to and from Nutgrove. Unusually, there were no fixed stops on part of the route. To reach the depot in St. Helens, one trolley arm was placed on the tramway overhead and a skate attached to a chain was dragged along the tram track to give a negative return. This method was used elsewhere but St. Helens is the only known case where passengers were carried. Through motor buses were run between St. Helens and the Cable Works for their employees.

The public liked the trolleybuses and it was decided to convert the Parr route which was extended along Derbyshire Hill Road to Platt Street (now Waring Avenue). Motor buses ran temporarily from 9th December 1928 and trolleybuses took over the route on 30th July 1929.

Interurban Services

Agreement was reached with Lancashire United for a jointly operated bus service between Earlestown and St. Helens which started on 1st September 1927, the first of many joint services. Agreement with the road authorities enabled the Eccleston buses to be extended to the old post office and to Bleak Hill and the Haresfinch-Prescot service via Dentons Green, Eccleston and Gillars Green started in May 1928.

Bell negotiated with Lancashire United and Ribble for services to Warrington and Southport and a through service between those places, run by all three operators, started on 28th June 1928, absorbing the Corporation's Burtonwood and Rainford routes. It was unusual for a municipal transport undertaking to participate in a 30-

Number 6 was one of a pair of Guy BB 32-seat buses delivered in April 1925 and was decorated for the May Day celebrations.

mile long inter-urban route, which was destined to carry thousands of passengers over the next few years.

Corporation buses were run to Rugby League matches in Wigan, Leigh, Widnes and Warrington and also on private hire trips to Southport and even Blackpool. This annoyed the local charabanc operators who felt that this was stretching the 'in extension of any tram route' clause unduly. It seems that the Town Clerk was a little uneasy about that, too. The local coach operators lacked the financial resources to mount a full scale legal action which might have gone to the House of Lords but, because of their own doubts, the Corporation agreed to talks. The result was that the local operators agreed not to challenge the Corporation's right to run buses to Liverpool, Ormskirk, Leigh and anywhere else within a 10-mile radius from the Town Hall while the Corporation handed over its long distance bookings and agreed private hire rates. The Wigan Coach-owners Association was nominated as arbitrator in any future dispute.

Bell did not neglect the trams and a through service between St. Helens and Wigan via Ashton was run jointly from April 1927, after SLT had laid a new curve, though it was confined to weekends only from August because of delays caused by limitations of the single track between Ashton and Wigan and withdrawn after 27th May 1928. At the end of 1927, SLT terminated the agreement whereby St. Helens had worked the Haydock-Ashton section since 1909 and, from 18th June 1928,

A 1919 Leyland, believed to be an N type, acquired with the business of the St. Helens & District Motor Service Co. Ltd. in 1927. It became No. 14 in the Corporation fleet (later No. 60) and was withdrawn in November 1931. The official records say that the body was by Leyland but it has the appearance of being by E. & A. Hora who are known to have supplied bodies to the St. Helens & District company during the 1914-18 war.

the St. Helens-Ashton service was worked jointly. Liverpool Corporation was hostile to a through St. Helens-Liverpool tram service, claiming difficulties due to different rail sections and wheel profiles. But Liverpool was obviously the prize and Bell applied for bus licences to run an hourly service through to Canning Place, at first by extending the Haresfinch-Prescot service and later from the town centre in association with Lancashire United who wished to extend their Leigh service, by now running through to Salford. St. Helens also planned a bus service to Wigan via Garswood to avoid the tram tracks as far as possible. In April 1928, Ribble obtained licences in Liverpool and Wigan for an express service between the two places but St. Helens would not grant permission for people to be picked up in the town. Liverpool Watch Committee refused the St. Helens Corporation application and an appeal was lodged with the Minister of Transport.

In the meantime, Liverpool reduced the Prescot-Liverpool tram fare from 6d to 4d and through tickets at 7d were issued between St. Helens and Liverpool, changing trams at Prescot. Liverpool's thinking was that no bus operator would want to compete with such a low fare which was also below the cheapest railway fares. There was then a change of heart and a half-hearted attempt was made at a through tram service, worked hourly by two Liverpool cars between St. Helens and Lime Street from 13th December 1928, the day before the Ministry's Inquiry began. It was slow, erratic and prone to delays from other cars and ceased after

The St. Helens & District company had split in 1919, the charabanc business subsequently being carried on as Marshall Garages some of whose Daimler vehicles are shown on this Widnes Conservative Ladies' outing in 1920.

As the buses started to run further afield, St. Helens Corporation came into conflict with the local coach operators. This Leyland of James Bridge & Son was typical of the vehicles still being run by the local operators in the mid- and late-1920s though many were fitted with pneumatic tyres.

A rare view of St. Helens Corporation's first trolleybus at work on the A57 Warrington-Liverpool road after being renumbered from 1 to 101 in 1929. This was one of four Garretts with Ransomes bodies supplied in 1927.

three months, allegedly because the St. Helens police made difficulties about licensing the Liverpool cars, drivers and conductors.

The appeal to the Minister was dismissed and there followed a period of lengthy negotiations between Wigan and St. Helens Corporations and Ribble, the latter agreeing in principle to three-way joint operation between Wigan and Liverpool via Billinge. However, in October 1930, Ribble learned that Wigan, St. Helens and Lancashire United were planning a Wigan-Liverpool service via Platt Bridge and Haydock and immediately started their Wigan-Liverpool express service via Billinge on 25th October 1930, picking up only return ticket holders in St. Helens to circumvent the absence of licences as far as possible.

Bell left in November 1928 to become general manager of the Yorkshire Woollen District company at Dewsbury but he had already laid down the framework of very successful motor- and trolleybus systems at St. Helens. His successor, Ben England, also came from the West Riding company and continued the good work. He wanted to run the whole of the Prescot tram service through to Liverpool but Liverpool Corporation was not interested. The whole question of bus services to Liverpool was in abeyance pending the introduction of national road service licensing in 1931.

A Joint Trolleybus Service

In August 1930, SLT converted their Ashton-Atherton route to trolleybus operation and, as it was now isolated from the rest of the company's tramways, St. Helens Corporation once more took over the St. Helens-Ashton tram service. On 21st June 1931 a through trolleybus service started between St. Helens, Haydock, Ashton, Hindley and Atherton (13.89 miles), operated jointly by St. Helens Corporation and the South Lancashire Transport Co. For a time, this was the longest trolleybus service in Britain with a journey time of 75 minutes. In addition, St. Helens ran intermediate trips to the Huntsman at Blackbrook and the Ram's Head at Haydock where reversing facilities were provided.

Although the Council had not formally declared a policy of total tramway abandonment, it now seemed certain that this would happen but the large sums spent on the tramways in the 1920s made it necessary to get more life out of them. When getting powers for the Parr and Blackbrook conversions, authority had also been obtained to convert the Windle route, with an extension to Moss Bank, provide a new route along Eccleston Street and Knowsley Road to Dunriding Lane and extend the Parr route to the borough boundary, both along Newton Road and Fleet Lane.

Symbolic of change, Ransomes trolleybus 108 of 1929, en route to Parr is see with low-height car No. 9 (formerly 15) heading for St. Helens Junction. Trams and trolleybuses shared the same overhead so there was no overtaking.

THE 1930s

The Interurban Services

The Traffic Commissioners almost certainly persuaded the operators to get together and come to some agreement about the interurban services, failing which they would have imposed their own solution. A meeting held at Preston on 21st September 1931 was attended by representatives of St. Helens, Wigan, Leigh and Salford Corporations and the Lancashire United, Ribble and Crosville companies. The venue suggests that Ribble, an enthusiastic proponent of jointly operated services, took the initiative. The railways, who were concerned about loss of traffic, were large shareholders in both Crosville and Ribble and had made their views known beforehand, promising not to oppose any services which fell within their guidelines. They were not opposed to Liverpool-St. Helens-Wigan services. The meeting thrashed out the sphere of influence of each operator, Ribble's position having been strengthened by the signing of a zoning agreement with Liverpool Corporation which gave them a claim to the Liverpool-Prescot section. They agreed to admit St. Helens Corporation as a partner in their Liverpool-Billinge-Wigan express service which was to become 'local' over certain sections and to the establishment of a new Liverpool-Wigan service via Ashton and Platt Bridge in which Lancashire United, St. Helens and Wigan

Corporations would also participate. The Lancashire United Salford-St. Helens service was to be extended to Liverpool and shared by five operators – Ribble, Lancashire United, St. Helens, Leigh and Salford Corporations though, by agreement, it was run by Lancashire United buses.

All these proposals were put into effect in 1932 and from 1st May 1933, the three Liverpool services were co-ordinated to give a half-hourly service between St. Helens and Liverpool, all tickets to be interavailable. Wigan Corporation buses started to run through to Liverpool on the service via Ashton in November 1935. Meanwhile talks had been going on between Ribble, St. Helens and Wigan Corporations about the status of the stopping service between St. Helens and Wigan via Billinge over which St. Helens buses ran as far as Billinge. On 11th August 1935, the three operators jointly took over Cadmans Services who ran between Wigan and Rainford via Billinge and revenue on these services was pooled. St. Helens buses now ran through from St. Helens to Wigan but Wigan Corporation buses

Garrett centre-entrance trolleybus No. 1 (later 101) stands at the Prescot terminus in Warrington Road where there was a very tight turning circle by the Co-op Stores.

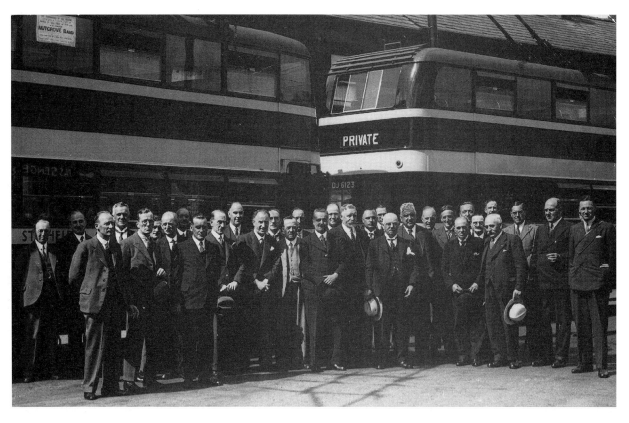

The civic party on the occasion of the opening of the St. Helens-Nutgrove trolleybus link on 4th July 1934 with trolleybuses 117 and 125 in the background. The current general manager, A.A. Jackson, is in the centre, holding a bowler hat.

normally only ran when there was a rugby match in St. Helens. The St. Helens-Carr Mill service was included in the pool from 1936.

St. Helens Corporation wanted to establish a through service to Widnes but the LMS railway was strongly opposed, maintaining that its service was quite adequate. Widnes Corporation had run a few buses to the boundary at Bell Lane, Sutton Manor since July 1921 and, to thwart railway opposition, it was agreed to apply to the Traffic Commissioners to extend them to St. Helens, withdrawing some trips between Sutton Manor and St. Helens so that the total facilities remained the same. This was eventually granted and a rather poor service was started on 5th April 1934. It was nominally jointly operated but the times granted were such that it could be

run by one Widnes bus. The first trip from St. Helens was at 4.0pm!

More Trolleybuses

In 1933, St. Helens Corporation sought further powers to run trolleybuses but was only partly successful as Whiston Rural District Council opposed the erection of wires in Eccleston. The Corporation envisaged extending the Dentons Green route via Kiln Lane to Eccleston, returning to town via Knowsley Road and vice versa, also a link along Hard Lane between Dentons Green and Windle City. Loops at St. Helens Junction and Prescot were also needed. Only the sections within the borough and at Prescot were granted.

Plans to replace the Windle City trams by trolleybuses

Ransomes 3-axle trolleybus 114 is en route to Atherton along Church Road, Haydock when new, the only other traffic being a now vintage Austin car. The single tram track is still in place in the roadway.

A busy prewar scene at Sefton Place with Leyland TBD2 No. 122 loading for Prescot on the island and another vehicle, bound for St. Helens Junction, on the left. A conductor finishing duty, dressed in summer dust coat and white topped cap, carries his ticket box towards the depot while the drivers exchange views. The overhead was not joined at this point. Tram track can still be seen in the road so the picture probably dates from 1936-37.

extended to Moss Bank were also frustrated by Whiston RDC who wanted St. Helens Corporation to pay for road improvements. The Windle trams were replaced by the first diesel buses, Crossley double deckers, which continued to Moss Bank station, in July 1932. Part of the disputed route went into the borough when the boundary was extended and trolleybuses, running through to Parr, replaced the diesels from 16th May 1934. The trams to Nutgrove were replaced by trolleybuses in July 1934, and a through service was run between St. Helens, Rainhill and Prescot, using double-deck vehicles, the single-deck trolleybuses being relegated to peak hour duties. The Prescot trams and the Rainhill trolleybuses

provided a five-minute service between the town and Toll Bar.

In 1935, it was decided to convert the St. Helens Junction and Dentons Green routes; the former changed over on 1st May and the latter four weeks later, the through service being reinstated. Only the direct Prescot service was now run by trams, the fleet being reduced to eight cars. The council fixed 31st March 1936 as the last day for the trams. A special last tram (No. 26) ran for members of the council and officials on 1st April from which day a circular trolleybus service ran between St. Helens and Prescot via Eccleston Park, returning via Rainhill and vice versa. A short length of St.Helens-

Ransomes D4 No. 120 (DJ 6055) with Brush 50-seat body, sports a route board for the Moss Bank-Parr through service when pictured turning from Cotham Street into Baldwin Street. These boards, apparently favoured by the incumbent general manager, A.A. Jackson, were short-lived.

Two Brush-bodied trolleybuses, Ransomes No. 117 and Leyland 125, were used to convey the civic party on the extension of the original Prescot-Rainhill line into St. Helens on 4th July 1934, thus linking up the separate parts of the trolleybus system. The scene is the Reform Club, Prescot.

owned track remained in position in St. Helens Road, Prescot for use by Liverpool's trams, for the next 13 years.

Local Motor Bus Services

It will be realised that, except on the inter-urban routes, the motor buses were employed in a secondary capacity but their role increased gradually as prosperity slowly returned in the 1930s. A Saturday service to Crank and Kings Moss started in February 1932; in August it became a daily service and it was extended by a lengthy rural route via Rainford, Mossborough and Gillars Green to Prescot on Saturdays and Sundays during the

summer. The Sutton Manor route was run by double-deckers and increased in frequency several times, more and more buses serving Sutton Leach en route. Some Gorsey Lane buses were extended to Bold Heath on Fridays and Saturdays in 1932 and, from 1936, this was run on summer Sundays also though the Monday service to Gorsey Lane was discontinued because of poor patronage. The Sutton district was given a new circular service on Fridays, Saturdays, Sundays and Mondays in 1937. It started at Market Street and ran via New Street, Sutton Leach, Sutton Road and Peasley Cross back to Market Street and vice versa.

From 1935 a bus ran between Victoria Square and the Cemetery via Windle Street and Bishop Road on Sunday afternoons, the last bus running earlier as the days got shorter. This continued until the outbreak of war. The Eccleston services were increased in 1936 with buses running to Bleak Hill via both Liverpool Road and Eccleston Street

Leyland TBD2 trolleybus No. 127 turns from Corporation Street into Hall Street for the depot. Its Massey Bros. lowbridge body was almost identical to the Brush body on No. 116 (left). The man in a trilby smoking a cigarette was Job Preston, Rolling Stock Superintendent for many years until his sudden death in July 1946.

The Sutton Manor route, bought from the St. Helens & District company in 1927, terminated in Market Street, beside the Parish Church. Leyland Titan TD1 No. 70 is shown at the terminus (above) and also passing under Peasley Cross bridge. Note the injunction to upper-deck passengers on open-top trams to 'Please Keep Your Seats' and the raised footpath, designed to keep the feet of passers-by dry when the road flooded beneath the bridge.

and via Virgil Street and Cambridge Road also to the Griffin Inn. As traffic increased, buses were taken off the narrow side streets and rerouted along Boundary Road in 1939.

A Friday service to Sutton Heath via Sherdley Road was provided from December 1935 and in 1937 an hourly St. Helens-Prescot service via Sherdley Road, Elephant Lane, Grange Park, Portico and Whiston started, running daily.

Prosperity Returns

With a greater demand for coal, more miners were needed and colliery services to Bold, Clock Face, Sutton Manor, Lea Green and Essex Street (for St. Helens colliery) were augmented. A new service from Finger Post to Sutton Manor colliery via Gaskell Street started in 1938. Some of these buses ran from as far afield as Rainford, Far Moor and Billinge. Other services from the country districts were run by coach operators.

More buses were run to B.I. Cables and, although there was a turning circle outside the works, the trolleybuses were augmented by motor buses. Increasing employment brought more traffic to all the services and frequencies were increased and extra buses run, particularly at weekends.

Replacement of trams by faster and more comfortable trolleybuses encouraged travel and routes such as Prescot with 10-minute frequencies in 1933 were being run every six to eight minutes in 1939. The Eccleston motor bus services, half-hourly in 1933 were three times as frequent in 1939. Many of the advertised services were augmented by unadvertised extras such as the Friday and Saturday services to the Huntsman and Haydock, Ram's Head.

Leyland TS6c No. 58 with English Electric body came to grief during the hard winter of 1947. The setting of the destination screen suggests that it was not on service at the time, possibly running as a staff bus. During the repairs, the body was refurbished, the nearside canopy being cut away and new destination and route number indicators fitted. It was renumbered 261 and remained in service until December 1950.

Titan TD5c No. 85, one of four entering service in June 1938, shows off the sleek lines of the Leyland pre-war lowbridge metal-framed body to perfection. Note the revised livery, using more cream, and the removal of the fleet title from the waistband to the lower panels. These buses had compressed air bells and were regular performers on the Sutton Manor service but also ran to Liverpool. This bus lost its torque-convertor after the war and was briefly renumbered 54 before sale for scrap in October 1955.

Cheap Fares

Tram and trolleybuses services, with a high initial capital cost, relied on high residential density to enable them to provide cheap transport but many roads in St. Helens had little depth to the housing, a feature compounded by the large areas set aside for industry. This resulted in fares being higher than in some neighbouring towns and invited invidious comparisons from the public. It was not until July 1935 that 1d fares were generally charged on all routes; hitherto the minimum fare had been 1½d except for a few specially selected short stages. But St. Helens had a tradition of issuing cheap return tickets throughout the day, a facility which was offered by very few municipal operators. Fares were reduced generally throughout the 1930s, culminating in a general reduction from 2nd July 1939 when it was said that one million additional passengers were needed to ensure the continuation of the new low fares. Unfortunately, the outbreak of war two months later brought this experiment to a premature end.

St. Helens was particularly generous at providing cheap fares for schoolchildren. The age of eligibility for half fares was raised from 12 to 14 in January 1929 and, the following year, a new scale of children's fares gave the benefit of some fractions to the passenger. Children's 2d return parks tickets were available within the borough during the summer holidays to and from any park and a ½d child's fare for 1d stages was approved in September 1935. In 1938 a 1d school return ticket was introduced for trips wholly within the borough including break of journey facilities. For journeys outside the borough, weekly contracts were issued at five or six times the adult single fare.

Workmen's fares were generally issued up to 8.30am at single fare for the return journey and, to cater for shift workers, special weekly tickets were available Although through tickets to Liverpool by tram were withdrawn when the last trams came off in 1936, one could still buy cheap New Brighton ferry tickets and admission tickets to Liverpool Zoo from trolleybus conductors.

THE 1939-45 WAR

During the summer of 1939, when war seemed imminent, plans were made for rationing motor fuel as, at that time, there was no domestic supply, and all fuel would have to be imported across seas infested by enemy naval craft. Motor bus operators were told to draw up time-tables to save 40% of their fuel but tram and trolleybus services, powered by home-produced electricity, were exempt. However, many trolleybus operators seem to have had their motor bus services reduced more savagely than those with all motor bus systems and St. Helens was no exception. After war was declared on 3rd September 1939, cuts in services had to be implemented within three weeks. St. Helens' reduced motor bus services were mostly put into effect on 18th September with very severe cuts.

Services withdrawn altogether included the Sutton Leach circular, Prescot via Sherdley Road, Gorsey Lane and Bold Heath (except for one early journey), Haresfinch-Prescot and the special Sunday routes to the Cemetery and Sutton Heath, the latter having buses only on Fridays and Saturdays. The government wanted to discourage pleasure travel so the Southport service was curtailed at Ormskirk, Kings Moss confined to Saturdays only (and the Prescot extension cancelled) and the Liverpool-Wigan via Billinge service withdrawn.

Frequencies were reduced on remaining services and late buses cancelled as there was little or no demand.

Initially, all places of entertainment were closed as it was thought that there would be widespread air raids; the blackout was virtually complete and few people wished to venture out at night. The joint Atherton trolleybus service was split at Haydock during the late evening, each operator keeping to its own territory.

Many of the transport staff were called up for the forces immediately but the service reductions enabled the department to cope adequately though the employment of conductresses was approved. The most serious problems were caused by the blackout. Headlamps and interior lights had to be masked to show the minimum of light and measures taken, as far as possible, to prevent flashes from the overhead. Mudguards, platform edges and handrails were painted white and white bands were painted on street furniture and kerb edges. Reduced services meant higher average loadings and the need to enforce queuing, and barriers were erected at several town centre loading points. The Sefton Place departure point for the Prescot and Rainhill

Wartime Sunbeam MF2 trolleybus 157 (DJ 9005) passes along Prescot Road en route for Rainhill and Prescot. Note the wartime masked headlights and white paint round the mudguards and lifeguards. Route numbers only were carried on the front with the destination shown on the nearside. The front destination equipment was altered during post-war body overhaul.

trolleybus services, in the centre of the junction, was hazardous under blackout conditions and it was transferred to Bridge Street.

Wartime problems were compounded in January 1940 by the most serious blizzard for 40 years. All services were suspended for a time, trolleybus routes having to be reopened by motor buses, some of which ran with snow chains inside the borough for the first time ever.

As in most towns, initial service reductions proved to be too severe and new motor bus time-tables came into effect on 4th February 1940. Extra buses were run to Alder Hey Road to supplement the hourly Bleak Hill and Griffin Inn buses and more buses to Sutton Leach and Sutton Manor were approved.

New Industrial Services

Industry was gradually adjusting to wartime needs. All the collieries were in full production and many factories went on to shift working. With so much extractive and heavy industry employing only men, St. Helens had a pool of female labour available for production work and, as new war factories were opened, a need arose for transport facilities for these workers. In 1941, labour was recruited in St. Helens for the Royal Ordnance Factory, built north of the East Lancashire Road on Simonswood Moss, which became known as ROF Kirkby and a workers' shift service was run via Eccleston and Bleak Hill; it was followed by another service to and from the Napier Factory on the East Lancashire Road at Gillmoss, which ran via Dentons Green.

Many extra colliery buses were needed and more labour had to be drawn from further afield. Cronton Colliery, which had been served mainly by private coach operators, recruited men in the Wigan area and, by May 1941, a new joint service was being run, mainly by Ribble, from Lamberhead Green, through Billinge and St. Helens to the colliery. By January 1943, a shuttle was running between Whiston and the colliery in which St. Helens buses participated. The Burtonwood Repair Depot, situated at a large new RAF station at Burtonwood, (euphemistically styled 'Sankey BRD') provided employment for hundreds of civilian workers from surrounding towns. The first service, from Foundry Street via Leach Lane and Clock Face started on 17th November 1941 and eventually a network of routes was established. In March 1942 the site was handed over to the US Air Force and by 1945 there were 14,000 airmen and 4,000 civilians on the base. These services were treated as part of the Warrington-Southport pool and, while most of the work was done by St. Helens Corporation, there was some LUT participation.

Other industries for which labour was recruited in St. Helens were located in Widnes and Warrington and services to the Everite Works and to Widnes centre were augmented during 1942-43 with journeys via Bold Heath in addition to the established route via Sutton Manor. Double-deck buses were now needed and Widnes Corporation obtained three lowbridge Daimlers which would pass under Warrington New Road bridge. A

workers' service from St. Helens to Warrington via Clock Face and Bold Heath commenced on 19th March 1944.

Trolleybus Services

At the outbreak of war, the 52 trolleybuses comprised 57% of the total municipal bus fleet but they carried a much higher proportion of the traffic, being employed on the principal all-day services. The main exception was the Eccleston route which had been authorised for trolleybus operation before the war and, in August 1941, the general manager, by this time W.M. Little, proposed that authority should be sought to make the conversion in order to save fuel. A turning circle at Parr Library was also suggested as many passengers on the Parr route travelled only a short distance and voltage drop at the end of the line was a problem.

Both these proposals were approved and the work was done by direct labour, a major undertaking under wartime conditions; some second hand poles were used. The department had started the war with large stocks of overhead equipment and long stretches of overhead line had been renewed on the Prescot circle during 1939-40. The Parr Library turning circle came into use in 1942 while work on the Eccleston route continued slowly as labour and material became available. When 8ft wide trolleybuses were taken into stock in 1942, it was found necessary to install a new turning loop at Prescot. Overhead was erected in Grosvenor Road and Wycherley Street so that the reversing manoeuvre was eliminated. This used up more material needed for the Eccleston route which eventually came into use on 29th June 1943. The new line left the Dentons Green route at the Lingholme Hotel and extended along Boundary Road and Knowsley Road to Ackers Lane with a turning circle at Dunriding Lane to serve the Rugby League football ground. The trolleybuses operated through to Shaw Street railway station. The motor bus service to Alder Hey Road was withdrawn, the hourly Bleak Hill and Griffin Inn buses being diverted via Liverpool Road and Eccleston Street instead of Boundary Road.

In 1942, the general manager had suggested that route numbers be adopted and these were allocated to trolleybus services initially in June of that year. The 8ft wide utility trolleybuses were fitted with large screens at the front bearing only numbers but it was some time before numbers were displayed on the older vehicles, though trolleybuses rebuilt from 1944 onwards were equipped with number boxes instead of intermediate screens.

Ironically, in April 1944, the Regional Transport Commissioner ordered a reduction in trolleybus services following a directive from the Ministry of Fuel and Power designed to prevent power cuts because of an electricity power shortage and frequencies were reduced accordingly.

The Later War Years

On Sundays during the summer, buses on certain routes were likely to be packed with people looking for some

relief from their wartime problems by making day trips to New Brighton, Southport or places in the countryside. Evening local buses would be swamped by returning excursionists to the exclusion of shift workers. To discourage this kind of travel, further restrictions on interurban services were imposed from 27th July 1942. The Sunday services on all the Liverpool routes were withdrawn altogether and the Warrington-Ormskirk service was split at St. Helens. Last buses on the town routes were run at 10.15pm and special permits were issued to late workers giving them priority over ordinary passengers. In November 1942, the Regional Transport Commissioner asked for a further 10% cut in motor bus services which the Corporation felt was impracticable but some saving was achieved by running last buses at 9.45pm. Proposals to run trolleybuses until 10.45pm ran into trouble as it was difficult to justify running late buses on some routes and deny them to those who lived on motor bus routes, for which there was no fuel. With an improvement in the fortunes of war, the services to Sutton Manor, Carr Mill, Bleak Hill and Rainford were increased in December 1943. From 2nd April 1944, all motor bus services ran to and from Victoria Square and trolleybus services from the streets adjoining Sefton Place or from Bridge Street.

Although St. Helens experienced no large scale aerial attack, it suffered from being so close to Liverpool. The overhead line section's crews did valuable work in Liverpool to help restore tram services after the eight-day air raids in May 1941. The fear of a bomb hitting the depot was met in St. Helens, as in many other towns, by dispersing vehicles at night and trolleybuses stood in City Road near Victoria Park, Baldwin Street and near

Leyland trolleybus 130 (DJ 6457) is seen in Blackbrook Road with its new East Lancashire body fitted in August 1945.

Shaw Street station, resulting in a serious deterioration in the body condition of the older vehicles, and an extensive refurbishment programme was authorised in October 1942. Extra vehicles were needed for the Ackers Lane service and to replace the worn out single-deckers and three-axle buses; ten trolleybuses built on chassis originally intended to be exported to Johannesburg were allocated to St. Helens by the Ministry of War Transport as described in Chapter 8. A number of utility motor buses were also received and two buses were hired from Bolton Corporation. By early 1945, the fleet had increased to 60 trolleybuses and 51 motor buses. With lighting restrictions relaxed and the war in Europe going well, plans were made for improved services.

Wartime conditions taught the bus operators many lessons about co-operation with each other. Whereas there had been a desire to participate in all joint services for reasons of civic pride, it was realised that it was often operationally convenient for one operator's mileage share on a particular route to be run off on another. Thus in September 1939, St. Helens buses ceased to participate in the Earlestown services and, to a great extent on the Wigan via Billinge service, too. It was much more economical for St. Helens to concentrate on the Warrington services with their heavy works traffic as neither Ribble nor Lancashire United had a depot conveniently located to operate these journeys and unnecessary dead mileage could not be tolerated under wartime conditions. To a large extent, these practices were continued after the war.

The Forces Leave Service

By 1945, the railways were running several special trains for servicemen coming on leave from Europe and two of these terminated at Liverpool (Lime Street) in the early hours of the morning. There was official reluctance to allocate fuel for buses to get these men home and various subterfuges were used. In Liverpool, vans were converted thus taking the problem outside the ambit of public service vehicle fuel rationing but it is not known how St. Helens got round the difficulty. The service, worked by volunteers, started on 27th August 1945 with two trips on six nights per week. On the seventh night, Liverpool Corporation provided transport to Prescot where servicemen transferred to cars provided by a local Volunteer Car Pool. Fares were 6d (2½p) to Prescot and 1/- (5p) beyond. Servicemen were allowed to use staff buses free of charge between St. Helens town centre and the suburbs. Understandably, large numbers of people were not carried, the totals for January and February 1946 being 228 and 208 respectively of which 64% travelled beyond Prescot. Nevertheless, these night buses gave an invaluable service to the men and they continued until the leave trains were withdrawn on 31st January 1947.

A Remarkable Achievement

The achievements of the St. Helens Corporation Transport department during the war have never been fully recognised. The problems created by wartime shortages were shared by all operators but the increase in traffic carried at St. Helens was nothing less than phenomenal. Comparing the last full pre-war financial year ended 31st March 1939 with the comparable period ended 31st March 1945, passengers carried had increased by 87% for a mileage increase of 12%. With no increase in fares, revenue had more than doubled though working expenses had increased by 76%. From a modest net revenue surplus of £20,238 in 1939, profits increased to £89,080 in 1945, a figure never attained again. This was achieved with a fleet increase from 94 to 111, (18%). Because of the cancellation of much non-essential mileage, vehicle utilisation fell from 35,006 to 31,488 miles per bus, a relief, no doubt to those doing their best to keep time-expired buses working longer. Average passengers carried per mile run increased from 7.05 in 1939 to 12.37 in 1945. This may seem a low rate of utilisation to the uninitiated but it must be borne in mind that many empty miles were run in connection with factory services and most peak hour traffic is essentially one way.

In the following table, 1939 figures are indexed as 100 and indices are given for the results in the war years.

WARTIME STATISTICS

Year Ended 31st Mar	Revenue £000s	Index	Working Expenses £000s	Index	Passengers 000s	Index	Mileage 000s	Index	Pence (d) per bus mile Revenue Index	Working Ex's Index
1939	168	100	128	100	22,951	100	3,256	100	12.35 100	9.43 100
1940	172	103	132	103	25,190	110	3,181	98	13.00 105	9.96 106
1941	209	125	151	118	27,656	120	3,009	92	16.65 135	12.02 127
1942	277	165	177	138	35,356	154	3,251	100	20.44 166	13.06 138
1943	303	181	201	157	38,435	167	3,344	103	21.77 176	14.40 153
1944	320	191	216	169	40,660	177	3,392	104	22.68 184	15.31 162
1945	345	206	239	187	42,872	187	3,464	106	23.87 193	16.56 176
1946	334	199	251	196	41,848	182	3,637	112	22.06 179	16.56 176

CHAPTER 6

1945-74

Mr G. W. Robb had succeeded W. M. Little as manager in February 1945 and it was to him and Joe Hoult, the traffic superintendent (later deputy manager) that the credit must go for the post-war expansion of St. Helens' bus services. The shortages and bureaucratic regulation of the post-war years were very frustrating and the new militancy of labour created constant problems for management. Nevertheless, residents in the St. Helens transport area experienced a progressive improvement in both the scope and the frequency of their services. A new depot had been proposed in Boardman's Lane in 1939 but this was now scrapped in favour of a parking ground in Jackson Street, opened on 2nd February 1947 and, eventually, in 1964, converted into a new garage. A comprehensive route number system was adopted for motor bus services and greater flexibility given to the trolleybus system by making minor improvements to the wiring. Some motor bus services were run over trolleybus services for a time because of inadequate power supply and four new sub-stations were installed using some equipment from the former Bury Corporation tramways. A sub-station was also built at Clinkham Wood, a new estate to the north of the East Lancashire Road, for which trolleybuses were proposed but never actually operated.

The collieries were very busy and labour was attracted from as far away as Liverpool, Bootle and Wigan whence special buses were run, mainly by Ribble but with some Corporation participation. The year 1946 saw new services commenced to Clinkham Wood (February), Grange Park, Huyton, Speke and Garston (May) and Sutton Leach (September). The Sutton Manor and Eccleston services were linked across the town centre, starting a policy which was more motivated by economies in operating costs than affinity of interests. There were insufficient resources to restart the Southport service for summer 1946 and it was the end of September before the Warrington-Southport through service was resumed. Extension of the Sutton Leach services to Clock Face and Bold all day in February 1947 brought frequent daily services to these areas for the first time.

Passing between the hospital walls, the highest numbered trolleybus, BUT 389 with East. Lancs. body, passes tower wagon DJ 7592, converted from a 1937 Leyland TS8 bus in April 1951. Route No. 9 indicated a bus terminating at Prescot and not passing round the circle, a practice which became regular following the introduction of motor bus route 96 in November 1957. Number 389 was sold to Bradford where it worked until 1971 when it was 20 years old.

The turning circle at Nutgrove enabled trolleybuses to terminate from either direction and short workings ran between Prescot and this point on Sunday afternoons, showing No. 9. From 1927 to 1934, passengers changed from tram to trolleybus or vice versa at this point. Sunbeam 375 heads for St. Helens and BUT 389 for Prescot via Rainhill on 31st March 1958.

An aerial view of 1945 Sunbeam W trolleybus 306 (DJ 9184) in Penny Lane, Haydock, en route from Atherton to St. Helens on 20th June 1956, emphasises the rural nature of this section of the route even at the end of trolleybus days.

A through Ackers Lane-Haydock trolleybus service started in May 1946, followed by an Ackers Lane-Parr Library service in November. The full potential of the trolleybus system was affected by shortages of vehicles and of power from time to time.

The new post-war mobility of labour brought new workers' services along the East Lancashire Road to Walton Hall Avenue, Liverpool for Littlewoods and other employers from February 1947 when services were started for the new BICC Rye Hey factory at Prescot. Similar facilities for the Melling factory followed in March 1948.

New Joint Services

Fuel restrictions on the Liverpool services were relaxed in November 1945 when Sunday services were restored. The frequencies of the three joint services were gradually built up to provide a combined 15-minute limited stop service to Liverpool. The Wigan-Liverpool via Billinge service, however, was resumed only on Saturdays and not until 1950. A dispute over the Speke and Garston services was settled in February 1947 by cancelling the Garston trips in favour of a half-hourly service to Speke which became joint with Crosville (and financially with Ribble also), Liverpool Corporation participation having been ruled out by the companies insisting on the rigid enforcement of a 1938 zoning agreement; this brought Crosville buses into the centre of St. Helens. A further joint service, involving Crosville and Warrington Corporation, was provided between St. Helens and Warrington via Clock Face and Bold Heath. Changes in educational arrangements brought Widnes Corporation buses into St. Helens via Rainhill on a new service for the R.C. Grammar School.

After competing applications had been submitted, St. Helens and Liverpool Corporations and Ribble agreed on a new St. Helens-Prescot-Kirkby service which started in June 1955 and was normally run by one St. Helens

Some of the South Lancs. Transport Company's 1930 Guy BTX trolleybuses, which worked the Atherton route from Platt Bridge depot jointly with St. Helens Corporation, remained in almost original condition to the end. Number 7 passes along Corporation Street on 31st May 1952.

It was rare for trolleybus overhead to be erected on unmetalled ground but this was done on 'the land', used for overflow parking in Hall Street. Wartime Sunbeam F4 No. 164 (DJ 9012), with Massey utility body, was extensively rebuilt in the Corporation workshops in 1948 and fluorescent lighting was installed experimentally.

Two highbridge Sunbeam F4 trolleybuses stand in Bridge Street outside the old Market Hall, on 21st May 1956 prior to working in opposite directions round the Prescot circle. Their bodies were built by East Lancs. Coachbuilders at their Bridlington factory. Both saw further service in South Shields after trolleybus operation in St. Helens ceased in June 1958.

Lambeth Street, Atherton was the easternmost place to which St. Helens trolleybuses worked, the distance from St. Helens being almost 14 miles. Roe-bodied Sunbeam W trolleybus 313 (upper) has just reversed across the main road. Another of the same batch, still numbered 114, prepares to turn left for the journey back to St. Helens.

bus. Another joint service, worked by one Corporation and one Crosville bus, started between St. Helens and Rainhill Stoops in April 1965.

New Housing

The growth of new housing estates led to constant pressure on the transport department for new and extended services and, at the same time, weakened the viability of the old-established trunk routes as residential density was lowered. In Clinkham Wood, buses served two (at one time three) routes and a separate service to Moss Bank Brow on the northern perimeter, which passed through Cowley Hill and Bishop Road en route. In 1950, the Bold and Gorsey Lane routes were linked to Clinkham Wood and the Sutton Heath service was extended to Sutton Manor, overlapping the service via Clock Face between Walkers Lane and Forest Road. A new service linked Ravenhead with Berry's Lane, Sutton across the town centre. New estates between Prescot and Whiston,

both north and south of Warrington Road were given new facilities.

The closure of the Widnes-St. Helens-Rainford railway line in June 1951 led to new and increased services between St. Helens and Widnes and also St. Helens and Rainford where the population was increasing. Construction of a new bridge during the final phase of Rainford by-pass enabled double-deck buses to be used on the Warrington-Southport and Rainford (Wheatsheaf) shorts from 1952. When the Rainford-Ormskirk train service was withdrawn in November 1956, the joint operators were surprised when a licence was granted for a Skelmersdale-St. Helens express service, not to them but to a coach operator, Gregson's (Motors) Ltd. It was not a success and was withdrawn in May 1960.

The Trolleybus System

In 1946, a licence had been granted for the Clinkham Wood motor bus service on the understanding that trolleybuses would be considered as soon as possible and in 1947 proposals had been drawn up to serve the estate and also to link the Dentons Green and Ackers Lane routes via Bleak Hill. The extension, being outside the St. Helens boundary, had been blocked by the Whiston Rural District Council. The railway also objected to wires over the level crossing at Moss Bank. Limited powers granted by an Act of 1948 were used only to the extent of wiring part of Claughton Street to form a turning loop in the town centre.

R. Edgeley Cox who had succeeded George Robb as general manager in June 1949 was an enthusiastic supporter of the trolleybus but in a frank report to the Transport Committee in March 1951 he stated that much of the trolleybus overhead was nearing the end of its useful life. Costs were increasing and stocks of overhead and other equipment salvaged from the worst affected routes could be used to maintain other parts of the system.

The Council decided upon the gradual replacement of trolleybuses by motor buses, basing their argument on changes in population density along the traditional main routes as people moved out to new housing estates. Buses already duplicated much of the trolleybus system and the cost of installing overhead wires could not be justified on routes of relatively low density. With the electricity supply nationalised, there was no longer an incentive to provide the municipal electricity undertaking with a captive consumer. Another factor, as wages rose every year, was the cost of keeping an overhead line crew on standby for about 20 hours a day. Higher diesel oil taxation almost led to a reappraisal of the policy late in 1953 but the programme went ahead and, in fact, was accelerated as the original target date for full conversion was 1961-62.

It was decided to withdraw trolleybuses from the Moss Bank, St.

Ransomes D4 No. 138, new in 1936, loads outside the Co-op in Sefton Place on the through Moss Bank-Parr service. The Massey body was extensively overhauled by Bankfield Engineering Co., Southport, the destination display being altered to the post-war standard. The bus carries the short-lived 'flash' livery of 1948-49. The municipal arms were applied lower and the word 'Transport' omitted from the undertaking's title. Number 138 was withdrawn in December 1950 and scrapped.

Snow still lies on the footpaths as Leyland TBD2 No. 101 passes beneath the Great Central bridge at Blackbrook en route to Haydock. Note the overhead, positioned close to the sides, above the footpaths, to avoid damage by any high vehicles.

Two Leigh Corporation Leyland Lion LT3s, with dual-entrance bodies built by Massey to a Leyland design, were hired for a year in 1947-48. They retained their blue livery but were given St. Helens fleet numbers 27-8. No. 28 (Leigh No. 44) is seen against Greenall's brewery wall (long demolished to make way for the Hardshaw Centre), awaiting its time to leave for Rainford with a Ribble utility Guy behind.

An unusual hire to beat the post-war bus shortage was of two normal-control Dennis Lancets from Northampton Corporation. They had 26-seat bodies by Grose and ran in St. Helens from September 1946 to July/August 1948. The red and cream livery was not inappropriate. Note the 'St. Helens Transport' board fixed to the nearside. Northampton's fleet numbers 55-56 were replaced by St. Helens numbers 25-26.

The post-war reconditioning programme produced some unusual combinations. Number 253 was originally 1935 Leyland TS6c 67 which was one of three fitted with new Roe dual-entrance bodies in 1950, their torque-convertors having been replaced by gearboxes. The passenger flow experiment was not a success and was soon abandoned. With a reduced demand for single-deck buses it was sold after three years, seeing further service in South Wales and another rebuild to forward-entrance layout.

Helens Junction, Dentons Green and Ackers Lane routes, replacing 20 trolleybuses with 15 motor buses. This was effected from 3rd February 1952 when the St. Helens Junction service was linked with Dentons Green and Eccleston, Moss Bank with Sutton Manor and an Eccleston circular service was inaugurated via Knowsley Road, Kiln Lane and Dentons Green as had been planned for trolleybuses. Cox bought London-type RT buses which were low enough to pass under Peasley Cross bridge.

The Haydock service was cut back to Sefton Place and the Parr service to Baldwin Street, with a new turning circle at Boardman's Lane for peak hour extras. The Parr route was served by trolleybuses until November 1955 when motor buses took over on a cross town service which absorbed the Eccleston circular. However, because of a vehicle shortage, two trolleybuses continued to run at peak hours, usually to Boardman's Lane but occasionally through to Waring Avenue, until 9th November 1956. A new housing estate was built and, from 1962, the Parr service became a circular at both ends, running alternately via Derbyshire Hill Road and Newton Road.

The South Lancashire Transport Co. was also scrapping its trolleybuses and the joint route to Atherton changed over to motor buses in November 1956. The Corporation's Haydock motor bus service was extended across the town to Hard Lane. This left only the Prescot

circle, worked by the newest trolleybuses and the public service ceased on 30th June 1958, with an official tour the following day. The electric bus with its rapid acceleration and almost silent progress had succumbed to the pressures of modern society.

Problems at Burtonwood

A government decision to extend the runway at the US Air Base at Burtonwood caused the closure of the road between Burtonwood and Sankey from 9th March 1953. This created enormous problems for the bus operators. At first the Warrington-Southport buses were rerouted via Bold Heath and Marshalls Cross, by-passing Burtonwood altogether except for a few trips over a very unsuitable road via Winwick, and the existing service via Bold Heath was reduced. But there were financial implications as Ribble and Lancashire United were the partners in the Southport service and Crosville and Warrington Corporation on the Bold Heath route. All the workers' services to the Air Base had to be rerouted so as to approach from the south, involving considerable extra mileage.

From September 1953, the Warrington-Southport service was rerouted via Burtonwood, Gorsey Lane and Bold Heath and the Winwick service withdrawn altogether. All the workers' services were recast in the light of the previous six months' experience. In the meantime, the County Council set about widening the

The acquisition of Bristol by the British Transport Commission cut off supplies to the municipal and private enterprise sectors and L6A No. 207 was one of the last such to be delivered in 1948 (201-8). Their AEC engines made them compatible with other vehicles in the fleet. These buses had Roe 35-seat rear-entrance bodies and 207 is seen on a private hire in Manchester in 1953, on loan to Gavin Murray, a local coach operator. Numbers 207-8 were withdrawn and sold prematurely in 1956 because fewer single-deck buses were needed but others ran until 1963-64.

Seen in Baldwin Street in St. Helens town centre, No. F101 was the first of nine Leyland PD2/20 buses delivered in 1955 with 61-seat East Lancs. four-bay bodies. Note the RT-style rear wheel discs which became standard in St. Helens for some years.

St. Helens Corporation buses were frequently hired by the local coach operators and AEC Regent III No. 31 of 1949 with 53-seat lowbridge East Lancs. body, is seen on a private hire in Manchester in 1953.

road and building new bridges between Burtonwood and Winwick and the Warrington-Southport service was diverted over this new road from 25th June 1955.

Leisure Services

In the post-war period, there was an enormous demand for transport to sporting events which continued for some years, declining slowly with the advent of private transport and television coverage. By virtue of its rare (for a municipality) excursion and tour licence, St. Helens Corporation was able to exploit the almost fanatical following of rugby league football with its excursions, run with double-deck buses, to the neighbouring towns who shared this enthusiasm. On the occasion of home matches, special motor buses were run from the town centre and Shaw Street station direct

Ribble Leyland PD2 with 61-seat Burlingham body passes the Ship Inn, Blackbrook on joint route 320 (Liverpool-Wigan) while passengers are transferred from failed Lancashire United Daimler 571 to Northern Counties bodied Guy Arab 619 on the St. Helens-Atherton joint ex-trolleybus service No. 1.

Crosville Bristol Lodekka MG887 passes St. Helens 7ft 6in wide Leyland PD2/22 with East Lancs. body at the Western Avenue, Speke terminus of joint route 89.

Joint services in action in Victoria Square, St. Helens. AEC Regent V 134 on a Parr to St. Helens short working overtakes all-Leyland Ribble PD2 2636 on the St. Helens-Liverpool joint service 317. The Ribble bus is waiting for Lancashire United Guy 551 to vacate the stand for the same service. The Guy is probably allocated to the company's Bentley Road, Liverpool garage.

to the Knowsley Road ground, at premium fares, in addition to augmented services on the Ackers Lane trolleybus route with through buses to and from St. Helens Junction for important matches. A turning circle at Dunriding Lane provided for special buses.

In 1956 when St. Helens reached the Rugby League final at Wembley, so many staff wanted to go to the match that the Corporation prevailed upon its joint operators to cover as many of its duties as possible on the inter-urban services. Crosville, Ribble and Lancashire United obliged and Liverpool Corporation ran the St. Helens-Prescot-Kirkby service, the only occasion that a Liverpool bus ran on service to St. Helens

Race meetings also provided plenty of passengers. Haydock Park racecourse lay adjacent to the Atherton trolleybus route, which would be augmented between St. Helens and Ashton, and the 320 Liverpool-Wigan route which gained patronage from further afield. The Spring meeting at Aintree was also very popular. Special buses were run to Waddicar, not far from the northern edge of the famous course on Jump Sunday and Grand National Day, using the route of the Melling works service. When, from 1951, Waddicar Lane became one-way during the meeting, this special service was diverted via Ribblers Lane (now largely stopped up since the M57 motorway was built) to Fazakerley.

The followers of greyhound racing also provided a lucrative source of off-peak traffic. The local track in Park Road was well-served by the Haydock services but, for important meetings, a dedicated service was run at a premium fare. Dog racing at Stanley track, Liverpool attracted hundreds of extra passengers despite the running of coach trips by the local excursion operators and it was common to see several St. Helens Corporation buses lined up in Prescot Road awaiting the conclusion of a meeting. When Liverpool sprouted a rugby league team which played at the same venue, there was even more traffic.

But the greatest leisure service of all was to Southport. Although it was a joint operation, the absence of Ribble or LUT depots anywhere near the town meant that the Corporation was left to provide the duplication from St. Helens and, on Whit Bank Holiday 1955, 32 duplicates were provided. Thereafter the Corporation cried 'enough' and a duplication schedule was prepared providing for participation of all three operators roughly in proportion to their shares in the service revenue.

Although perhaps not to be properly classified as a leisure activity, mention should be made of the special buses which ran to various Roman Catholic churches on Sunday mornings, waited during the service and then took worshippers home. Services of this kind were quite common in the more scattered parishes of South Lancashire and Ribble provided a great many of them. St. Helens Corporation was involved with at least four such services from 1958, serving St. Joseph's Church, Peasley Cross, St. Anne's Church, Monastery Lane and the Carmelite Convent, Eccleston.

In later years, a facility which enjoyed great popularity until the novelty wore off was to Knowsley Safari Park which ran during the school summer holidays, commencing on 3rd July 1971. Admission and a tour of the park were included in the fare and no doubt care had to be taken not to allocate an open-platform double-deck bus!

Decline

Many transport operators experienced their peak demand about 1950 when the post-war travel boom fizzled out but, in St. Helens, the peak year for passengers was 1955-56 when over 60 million were carried. Thereafter the decline, influenced by changes in social habits – in particular private transport and television – was inexorable, patronage falling to about 30 million in the final year of municipal operation.

Fares were kept at pre-war levels until 1953 when there was a modest increase and rises then came at regular intervals. The management

to Wigan.
Joint services in action in South John Street, Liverpool in December 1955. St. Helens 1949 AEC Regent III No. 27 with East Lancs. 53-seat lowbridge body precedes Lancashire United Guy Arab III 383 with lowbridge Weymann body, both on the 317 Liverpool-St. Helens service. Behind is Wigan Corporation all-Leyland PD2 No. 63 on the 320 service

A snowy scene in East Prescot Road, Liverpool with a Liverpool Corporation Leyland PD2 overtaking a long line of St. Helens buses operating in connection with a sports event. Guy Arab Mk II 92 (formerly 90) had lowbridge Weymann utility bodywork and had sliding windows, rear emergency window and route number fitted. Behind are two 1947 Leyland PD1s with lowbridge East Lancs. bodies. Note the radiused lower deck windows which were a feature of the Leylands and Bristols but not the AECs.

A busy scene in Ormskirk Street, St. Helens. Sunbeam trolleybus 375 bound for Prescot overtakes G118, a 1956 Leyland PD2/20 with 61-seat East Lancs. body, on the Haydock service while Bristol L6A 202 prepares to take up service in Bridge Street on the workers' service to Rye Hey Cable Works, Prescot.

RT No. 62, one of the original 15 was caught by the camera in Victoria Square on 2nd September 1950 while working the through route from Clinkham Wood to Gorsey Lane, Clock Face while AEC Regent III 31 loads for Sutton Manor.

Bristol K6A No. 50 with relaxed utility 1946 Strachan body was one of the last Bristols to have the high radiator. The difference between the high and low styles is clear from this view of 50 on training duty at Arpley Station, Warrington alongside Crosville Bristol KSW6B MW483, new in 1953.

kept fares down to a much greater extent than elsewhere. A comparison made in February 1968 revealed that a 1/- (5p) fare in St. Helens bought a ride of 7.75 miles while on the Burnley, Colne and Nelson joint municipal system it bought only 3.6 miles; on Ribble or LUT services it was worth only 2.5 miles.

The demand for school services following changes in the educational system added more mileage but little more revenue. This trend had started during the mid-1950s, the complex nature of dedicated school services having persuaded the department to introduce special route numbers starting at 601 in October 1956. School private hires, taking children to sports fields and swimming baths, were numbered from 500 up. This practice was copied by Liverpool Corporation some time later.

Closure of the Collieries

The rundown of the collieries and decline of heavy industry generally altered the pattern of the journey to work in St. Helens. During two specimen weeks in 1957, revenue from colliery services was 13.24d per mile with costs of 28.054d, an annual loss of £16,130. The longer colliery services, from Far Moor and Rainford, were withdrawn or severely reduced as early as 1957-58

and the decline in their patronage was steady. The Corporation cushioned the impact by negotiating guaranteed revenue agreements with the National Coal Board which made up the difference between fares paid and an agreed minimum revenue for each service. The opening of Parkside Colliery, Newton-le-Willows reversed the trend temporarily but, in February 1965, Lea Green colliery closed, some services then being curtailed at Ravenhead Colliery which also closed in October 1968. The longer services such as those from Liverpool and Wigan were replaced by contracts paid for by the National Coal Board.

The opening of Parr Industrial Estate in the late 1950s demonstrated the new trend but many of the new light industrial jobs were for women of whom there were now insufficient locally, special services, some subsidised by J & P Jacobs Ltd., coming from as far afield as Widnes.

Traffic Congestion

Another factor affecting reliability was traffic congestion. The first part of the ring road was opened in 1960 but, initially, the only buses to use it were football specials. All Prescot Road traffic was diverted outward via Borough Road instead of Croppers Hill from 31st August

AEC Regent II No. 39, followed by identical No. 36, loads for Widnes in St. Helens town centre when new in 1948. Note the original livery with red roof and the absence of trafficators, still not considered essential. Behind are a utility-bodied bus and an unrebuilt Leyland TS8.

Davies-bodied Leyland PD2/9 No. 77 leaves Southport bus station, followed by an all-Leyland Ribble PD2 en route to Preston. It is returning to St. Helens after working a duplicate journey. Note the resemblance to the Park Royal RT bodies, enhanced by the rear wheel-trims and small blind panel on the nearside lower deck.

The observer might be excused for believing that these two buses belonged to the same fleet. St. Helens Leyland PD2A/30 No. 13, new in 1962 with Metro-Cammell bodywork, passes Southport Corporation Leyland PS2/5 No. 12, new to Ribble in 1950 and cut down to open-top by Southport in 1964.

1964; this would have been a costly exercise if the trolleybuses had still been running as additional poles and overhead wires would have been needed.

However, the worst traffic hazard for the buses was crossing the East Lancashire Road when emerging from Clinkham Wood. Traffic moved at high speed and the dangers were such that, in fog, buses were diverted via Moss Bank. Eventually, the Moss Bank Road crossing, protected by traffic lights for many years, became intolerable and the problem was solved by converting the abandoned Rainford branch railway into a new road

(Scafell Road) and rerouting all traffic, including buses, from 3rd September 1973.

Labour Problems

For the last 25 years of its existence, the transport department was plagued by a shortage of drivers and conductors which got worse as more attractive employment with regular hours and free weekends became freely available. As early as 1950, service cuts were made in an effort to reduce the number of crew duties. In 1965 the shortage was 66 drivers and 32

St. Helens RT No. 24 (with tiny D-prefix below the nearside fleet No.), stands in Hope Street, Wigan awaiting time for departure on the 26-mile long route to Liverpool. It still has a single-roll route number blind. This route was jointly operated by Ribble, Lancashire United, St. Helens and Wigan Corporations. Today it survives, run by GM Buses North (successors to Lancashire United) but has lost its limited stop status.

Ten RTs line up in East Prescot Road, Liverpool having run in conjunction with a sports event. The last in line, No. 62, has an East Lancs. top deck, having lost the original in a low bridge accident in Southport on Whit Monday 1959. Number 337 was a Ribble-type designation invented by St. Helens Corporation for journeys turning short of the Liverpool terminus. It was chosen in the best tradition of associated Ribble numbers advancing in tens, 327 being in use elsewhere on the Ribble system.

conductors; three years later it was 64 drivers and 72 conductors. Services became unreliable and the loss of passengers accelerated. Drastic service cuts in September 1969 reduced the lost mileage from 9.84% to 1.33%. In the year ended 31st March 1969, over half a million scheduled miles were not run.

As wages and related expenses approached 70% of costs and staff shortages persisted, one-man operation was seen as a potential solution. It was believed that the payment of additional allowances to one-man operators would help to bring greater job satisfaction and reverse the drift of responsible workers away from the bus operating industry. Much patient negotiation was necessary before prejudices could be broken down. Negotiations covered not only extra payments but also design of vehicles, fare collection system, revised terminal arrangements to avoid reversing and additional journey time. The latter needed to be very carefully handled as submission to extravagant demands could cancel out the savings achieved by eliminating a conductor. Eventually the three 1963 AEC Reliances were converted and entered service as one-man vehicles in April 1967 on two lightly-trafficked routes, 22 Eccleston (Dodd Avenue)-Sutton (Lancots Lane) and 79 St. Helens-Rainhill Stoops.

The year 1967 was turbulent for labour relations in municipal transport generally. In October 1967, St. Helens, in common with many other municipalities, withdrew from the National Agreement, thus gaining freedom to negotiate wages and conditions locally. Nevertheless, there was soon an overtime ban in force followed by a two-day strike on 15-16th December. Shopkeepers, worried about losing their Christmas trade, provided free services using coaches hired in Manchester and other towns.

One-man operation of double-deck buses had been legalised in 1966 but, with current Union attitudes, it was not seriously considered in St. Helens. Instead, a policy of converting the fleet to dual-entrance single-deck with a high standing capacity was adopted and the AEC Swift, with 44 seats and accommodation for 20 standees, was chosen as the standard vehicle. Conversions then proceeded apace but usually after a dispute and a postponement on matters of detail.

Transport Act 1968

The Transport Act 1968 attempted to tackle some of the problems of road passenger transport. It created the National Bus Company into which both Crosville and Ribble were incorporated from 1st January 1969, though they retained their separate identities; it also established the first Passenger Transport Authorities, Merseyside

Two identical Marshall-bodied AEC Swifts stand in Bridge Street. No. 262, on route 96, dates from 1972 while 215, just visible behind on its way to Sutton Manor, was numerically the first of the type, delivered in June 1968.

Number 251 was a 1935 Leyland TS6c which received a new Roe 33-seat dual entrance body in August 1950, losing its torque-converter at the same time. In this form, it lasted until 1954 when it migrated to South Wales for further service with Jones Omnibus Services of Aberbeeg. It is seen in Bridge Street loading for Ravenhead.

being one of the first designated areas. The principle of subsidisation of socially necessary bus services by local authorities was given statutory support and grants were made available towards the cost of new buses, with a view to encouraging the changeover to one-man operation.

The Merseyside Passenger Transport Executive took over the Liverpool, Birkenhead and Wallasey transport undertakings on 1st December 1969. St. Helens, at this stage, was not involved directly but Prescot, Kirkby and some other outlying areas fell within the Passenger Transport Area and thus several St. Helens services became 'Area Bus Services'. However, matters were taken a stage further by the Local Government Act, 1972 which created the Merseyside County Council which was to become the transport authority. A new St. Helens Metropolitan Borough absorbed Rainford, Haydock and Newton-le-Willows. The St. Helens transport undertaking, together with that of Southport, was to be added to the existing Merseyside PTE fleet.

The inaugural date for the new County Council was

1st April 1974 so there was plenty of time to plan a smooth changeover. St. Helens was to become a semi-autonomous district within the PTE's existing Liverpool North division. To facilitate the change, the PTE requested the transfer of the St. Helens general manager, A.C. Barlow to the PTE as Divisional Manager, Wirral from 1st February 1973, the deputy general manager, L.H. Newall, being appointed in an acting role. In the months ahead, various decisions were made about the fleet to avoid waste, as described elsewhere.

At midnight on 31st March 1974, the St. Helens Corporation transport undertaking ceased to exist.

CHAPTER 7

THE TRAM FLEET

The Company Electric Cars

To commence operations, the New St. Helens & District Tramways Co. first ordered 16 cars from the British Thomson-Houston company who sub-contracted the order to the Brush Engineering Co. Ltd., Loughborough. They were of two types of which the smaller were 4-wheel cars mounted on Brill 21E, 6ft wheelbase trucks imported from USA, where the tramcar manufacturing industry was well-established. They were equipped with two 20 hp GE52-6T motors built by General Electric, Schenectady. The only BTH items on the cars were their K10 controllers. These cars seated 53 passengers, 24 inside facing each other on long wooden seats and 29 on reversible garden seats on the open top deck. The canopies were very short, leaving the driver completely exposed to the weather. The cars were singularly ill-equipped. Initially there were no destination indicators but, after some time, very small boxes were fitted, mounted on a long pole at each end of the upper deck. The cars had swivelling coupling bars and link-and-pin couplers, giving the erroneous impression that trailers were hauled. There were, at first, no lifeguards which were not at that time a legal requirement. There were a number of accidents and the practice was criticised. An early type of driver-activated device was unsatisfactory and, eventually, the more usual type of impact-activated guard and tray was fitted.

The larger cars were of similar general design but mounted on two Brill 22E maximum-traction bogies and the electrical equipment was by BTH. According to contemporary press reports they seated 67 passengers, 30 inside and 37 outside. The fleet numbering was curious, the small cars taking the odd numbers from 1-15 and the bogie cars the even numbers from 2 to 16. All the 4-wheel cars arrived in time for the opening in June 1899 but the bodies of the bogie cars were delayed until August.

A further 20 bogie cars were ordered from the British Westinghouse company but also sub-contracted to Brush; they were delivered in late 1899 and early 1900. They differed from the earlier bogie cars in having canopies which extended over the platforms and windscreens across their flat platform ends, a rare feature so early in the century. These screens did not extend round the offside of the car. They had reversed 'Mozley' stairs, designed by a man later well-known as the manager of Burnley tramways. Their seating capacity was probably 79, 36 in the lower saloon on longitudinal seats and 43 on the open top deck on pairs of reversible

Three four-wheel cars pass along Corporation Street and through Victoria Square in the early days of the electric tramways. The hoarding is believed to have been erected during the building of Queen Victoria's Diamond Jubilee statue.

Bogie car 19 is seen at Toll Bar where the Prescot and Rainhill routes diverged, the latter descending the hill to the left.

A view of part of the open top deck of a company electric car. Note the carpet overlays on the reversible slatted seats and the tiny destination indicator with 'Windle' displayed, probably on a glass slide.

Car 28 pauses at Huyton Lane, Prescot en route to Knotty Ash with Prescot parish church in the background. The Prescot Light Railway had several elaborate shelters and this one concealed electrical switch-gear. A proposed South Lancashire Tramways branch line down Huyton Lane to Broadgreen was never built.

Car 16, the last of the original bogie cars passes the old parish church while horse drawn traffic passes on both sides. Note the early electric street lamp suspended from the traction pole's bracket arm.

Number 5 as rebuilt in 1923 as a one-man car for use on the short Windle City route. If this is compared to the picture of the same car on page 11 it will be realised how extensive the rebuilding process was. Note the division of the saloon into two sections and the large 'Smoking' sign.

seats plus one odd seat abreast of the trolley mast. They were equipped with two Westinghouse controllers and two No. 38 motors and carried numbers 17-36.

All cars were fitted with swivelling trolley heads to the design of I.F. Cuttler. Fixed heads could not be used because, under low bridges, the overhead wires were mounted well to the nearside of the track to keep them out of reach of upper deck passengers.

Four of the 17-36 batch were withdrawn during the 1914-18 war, being probably de-motored to keep others on the road as parts for American equipment were in very short supply. The remains were almost certainly used as trailers for prisoner-of-war traffic by the South Lancashire Tramways Co. and then scrapped.

In 1918, four replacement open-top bogie cars were supplied by the English Electric Co. Ltd., Preston. In their original condition, these cars had traditional rounded ends and seated 74 passengers. It was extremely difficult to get new cars at this time and it is some indication of the dire straits of the St. Helens tramways that they were able to make a case for priority delivery. They were numbered 33-36 but it is possible that the

withdrawn cars had other numbers and some cars were renumbered to keep the new cars together in one group.

The Lancashire Light Railways Cars

The cars ordered for the Liverpool-Prescot Light Railway were kept at St. Helens and numbered on the end of the series. Numbers 37-41 were 4-wheel three-window saloon open-top cars with full canopies, built by G.F. Milnes & Co. Ltd., Birkenhead. They had Busch Waggonfabrik AG 6ft trucks and Belgian electrical equipment by S.A. Electricité et Hydraulique of Charleroi; they were part of a much bigger South Lancashire Tramways order. They were followed by two cars (42-43) built by the British Electric Car Co.; these had four-window saloons and short canopies and are thought to have been ordered by Aberdeen Corporation and rejected because they were too narrow. They were bought for £560 each in July 1902. Early records credit the LLR with the ownership of a single-deck car and this is believed to have been a small Milnes car built for the Atherton Bros. as a demonstrator for the Simplex conduit system which they endeavoured to promote

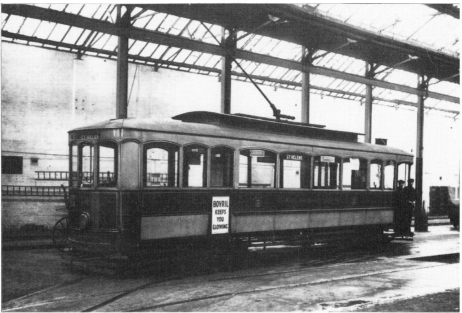

A depot shot of car 14, one of the two ex-Wigan bogie single-deck cars which clearly shows the clerestory and the internal bulkheads which revealed its origins as a combination car with open end sections. These cars ran in St. Helens on the Junction route from 1927 to 1935.

though they never considered it for any of there own schemes. A short length of track was laid down in Prescot cable works. It is thought that the car was intended to be used as a 'directors' saloon' but there is no record of its use and no one knows for sure what became of it.

Borrowed Cars

From time to time, the St. Helens cars were augmented by cars brought in from the neighbouring South Lancashire Tramways. Three of these which came in 1910 stayed at least six years and were given St. Helens numbers 44-46. Cars may have been exchanged at times and other SLT cars operated under their own numbers to meet emergency shortages. These were all four-wheel Milnes cars, similar to LLR Nos. 42-43. There were still three SLT cars in St. Helens at the time of the expiry of the lease and the Corporation hired them for a time.

New and Rebuilt Corporation Tramcars

The Corporation bought cars Nos. 1-36 but Nos. 37-43 were transferred to SLT where they became Nos. 83-89. In July 1919, the Corporation ordered four new cars from the Brush company and then increased the number to eight and specified windscreens. It was January 1921 before the order was fulfilled, the trucks, lower and upper decks being delivered separately and put together in St. Helens. The Brill 21E 7ft 6in wheelbase trucks were built by Brush. These were the first top-covered, balconied cars seen in St. Helens since the demise of the steam trailers and were much appreciated by the public. However, the Corporation were less pleased when they found they would not pass under Redgate bridge on the Haydock route. Ambitions for a fleet of new cars were ruled out on grounds of cost and the Corporation decided to renovate and rebuild with particular emphasis on covering top decks. Peasley Cross bridge was a worse

Bogie car 2 as rebuilt by the Corporation is seen at Prescot terminus. Note the domed top cover and the new style title on the waist rather than the rocker panels. These cars were withdrawn in 1934.

problem than Redgate and special measures were needed. The Council had overruled a committee decision to buy six single deck cars for the Junction route.

The programme was, of necessity, spread over a number of years. At least 17 car-sets of new BTH 40hp motors were purchased (1919-26); a tender for four more was accepted from Metro-Vick in 1920 and a further set was bought from the Sunderland District Electric Tramways which closed in 1925. Four top covers for 33-36 were bought from English Electric in 1920 and others from Yorkshire (West Riding) Electric Tramways in 1926 following the appointment of D.E. Bell from that company as manager. As time went on

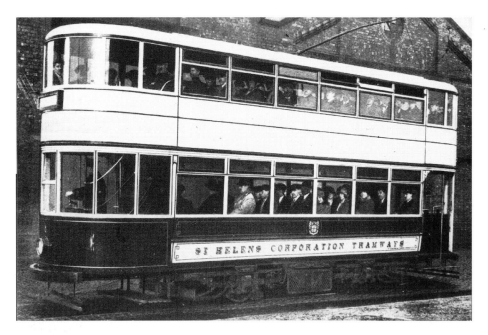

Car 1 as rebuilt as a fully-enclosed, low-height car with 10ft radial truck bears little resemblance to the original which was identical to car 5 shown on page 11. The depot background suggests that this was a council inspection on completion.

Fully-enclosed tram 15, bound for St. Helens Junction passes Leyland Titan TD1 70, inward bound from Sutton Manor near Peasley Cross.

and the Corporation's staff became more experienced, the rebuilds became more and more elaborate to the extent that some were virtually new cars but, as the Corporation had no statutory powers to manufacture, some part of the old car was incorporated so that it could be classed as rebuilt. The Rolling Stock Superintendent, W. Forber, designed a 10 ft radial truck (a four-wheel truck with play in the axles to ease its passage round curves). In 1923, car 5 was rebuilt incorporating this equipment, as a one-man single decker for the Windle City route while cars 1, 3, 7, 11, 14 and 15 also acquired it when rebuilt as low-height cars to pass under Peasley Cross bridge. They were 14ft 7in high with headroom of 5ft 11in in the lower saloon and 5ft 6in in the upper saloon. Domed roofs and open balconies with high railings were a feature of all these cars, except No. 1 which was fully enclosed. While bogie car 14 became a four-wheeler, car 7 was eventually mounted on bogies.

In 1927, two long bogie 1904-vintage single-deck cars were bought from Wigan Corporation; they were numbered 30-31, the cars of those numbers having been scrapped, together with 19. Numbers 9 and 13 remained open top and unrebuilt. Of the bogie cars, 2, 4, 6, 8 and 10 were all top-covered as probably were 12 and 16 though no record exists. Number 24 was converted to a works car and eventually ran unnumbered. In addition, there was an unnumbered rail-grinder. Of the new 1921 cars, all were eventually vestibuled and 42 was fully enclosed and received upholstered seats. It was used as the official last car.

In March 1929 the whole fleet – trams, trolleybuses and motor buses – was renumbered. Cars were withdrawn and scrapped each year from 1927 until, by 1936, only seven of the 1921 English Electric cars were left.

Livery

The first electric trams were painted a deep red, almost maroon, relieved by white for the waist panel, window frames and 'decency boards' along the sides of the top deck. About 1913, there was a change to green and white. The Corporation adopted a much brighter red with white relief and this continued to be applied in different combinations and with simplified lining-out throughout the life of the undertaking.

Car 26 (ex-42) a Brush car, new in 1921, was the only one to be enclosed on both decks and fitted with upholstered seats throughout. It is shown here with a trolleybus in a Last Tram ceremony on 31st March 1936.

The eight 1921 Brush cars were the last to remain in service and the cream upper works were painted in this rather attractive red style in the final years. The very high balcony railings were a feature of these cars. Car 28 (ex-44) is seen at the Dentons Green terminus in the final livery.

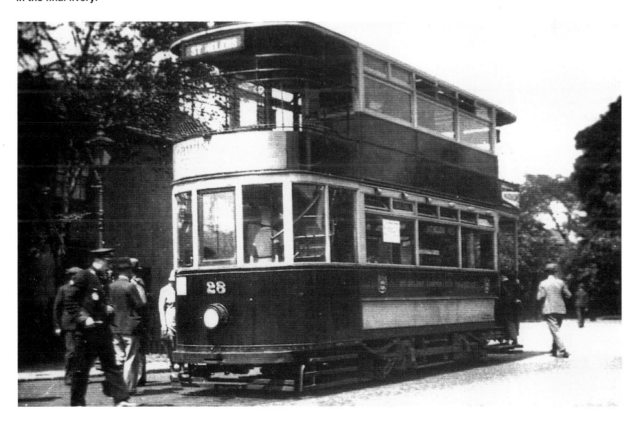

THE TROLLEYBUS FLEET

The Single Deck Vehicles

In the early years of the twentieth century, the trolleybus was perceived in Britain as a suitable vehicle for use on routes where the traffic potential was currently too low to justify the expense of installing a tramway. It used the same technology as the electric tramway and the law considered it to be a kind of tramcar. Early examples were trackless trams and 'the trackless' was always used in some towns rather than 'trolleybus'. The slow, solid-tyred vehicles were controlled by a tramcar controller, the driver steering with the right hand whilst working the controller with the left. By the time St. Helens adopted the mode, technical advances had put the trolleybus on pneumatic tyres, power being controlled by a foot pedal, and within a short time, trolleybuses were seen as electric buses rather than trackless trams, eminently suitable to replace time-expired trams.

Four centre-entrance single-deck trolleybuses (1-4) were ordered from Richard Garrett and Sons, Ltd. of Leiston, Suffolk, the first being delivered on tow on 13th June 1927. They were powered by one 50 hp Bull motor and had prominent cowcatcher style lifeguards. The 35-seat centre-entrance bodies by Ransomes, Sims and Jeffries of Ipswich had a high floor level with a mixture of longitudinal and transverse seating. Two 20 ft trolley booms were mounted one above the other on a common pivot. Choice of such small capacity vehicles to replace large tramcars gives some idea of the relatively light traffic but may also have been influenced by a weight restriction on the railway bridge at Thatto Heath which influenced vehicle policy for many years. This bridge had to be crossed when travelling to and from the depot.

A fifth vehicle of somewhat similar general design joined the fleet in July 1928. However, both chassis and 32-seat body were by Ransomes who also supplied the 50 hp series-wound motor. The electric equipment was by the Electro-Mechanical Brake Co. (EMB). This vehicle had a flatter roof and its appearance was improved by the absence of prominent lifeguards. It was originally numbered 5 but in the fleet renumbering of March 1929 it became 100, Nos. 1-4 taking the numbers 101-4.

For the conversion of the Parr route, a further five Ransomes vehicles with the same equipment as No. 5 were placed in service in July and August 1929. Their bodies were somewhat more modern in appearance with

The four original Garrett O type trolleybuses with 35-seat Ransomes bodies were lined up outside the Town Hall before entering service in 1927. Note the 'cowcatcher' lifeguards, seen as necessary in those days.

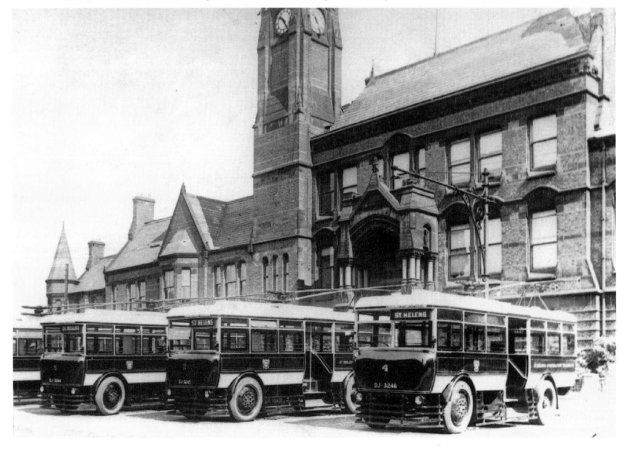

roof-mounted destination boxes at the front. They were numbered 105-9 though No. 109 did not arrive in St. Helens until November, having been used as a demonstrator at Rotherham where it was registered.

No. 100 (ex-5) was again renumbered 110 in February 1934. As further routes were converted, the single-deck trolleybuses became second line vehicles. Nos. 101-4 were withdrawn from regular service at the end of 1936; 102 was used as an illuminated bus both for the Coronation in 1937 and a Local Hospitals Campaign in 1938. Nos. 101, 103 and 104 were stored and re-entered service in October 1937 renumbered 161, 163-4, their old numbers having been taken by new vehicles in the meantime. They were finally withdrawn, together with 110, in July 1938 followed by 105-7 two months later. This left only 108-9 and, when war came, the general manager did not consider the centre-entrance arrangement safe in the blackout so they were withdrawn. All the single-deck trolleybuses were sold to Warburton of Warrington for scrap.

The Six-Wheelers

For the through joint service to Atherton, the Corporation obtained five three-axle trolleybuses on Ransomes D6 chassis with Ransomes lowbridge bodies seating 32 on the upper deck and 28 in the lower saloon (110-14). They were powered by two Ransomes 40 hp motors with one field, one armature, two separate windings and two commutators. Electrical equipment was by EMB. Like many trolleybuses of this period, they had three upper-deck front windows, an arrangement which gave greater strength to help carry the weight of the overhead equipment on the roof. They attracted some attention when new as they had a single-step entrance instead of the two-step arrangement common on many trolleybuses at that time. As the first was licensed from 1st March 1931, another from 1st April and all from 1st May, over six weeks before the Atherton service started, it seems likely that they saw some service on the Parr route but later they were confined to the joint service. No. 110 was renumbered 115 in February 1934.

By 1942, they had become unreliable and troublesome and all were withdrawn and stored on spare land in Tolver Street behind the depot. They were sold for scrap in August 1945.

No. 100 (DJ 3684) was originally numbered 5. It was the first all-Ransomes vehicle but as all the early single-deck trolleybuses in St. Helens were bodied by Ransomes they all had a family resemblance. Number 100 had a flatter roof than the earlier Garretts. It was again renumbered 110 in 1934 and withdrawn in July 1938.

The later Ransomes had the front destination box mounted centrally in the roof which improved their appearance. Number 106 (DJ 4082) was one of five (105-9) received in 1929 for the Parr route. The mounting of the two trolley arms one above the other on the same axis is clearly visible. This vehicle still has the 'Tramways' title shortly to be superseded by 'Transport'.

The Pre-War Four-Wheelers

Between May 1934 and December 1938, St. Helens Corporation took delivery of 45 two-axle double-deck trolleybuses all with lowbridge bodies seating 24 passengers on the upper deck and 26 on the lower deck. The upper deck seating was arranged in alternate rows of three and four seats in order to provide passing places along the sunken side gangway. Weight restrictions on various railway bridges limited capacity to 50. These vehicles came in six batches as follows:-

116-20   Chassis: Ransomes D4   Body: Brush.
                Motors: Ransomes 80 hp, series-wound,
                         series-field-regulated control
                Electrical equipment: EMB.

Number 120 was fitted with an EMB 80 hp motor at an unknown date. These vehicles had two-step platforms and a three-pane upper-deck front window. They were delivered in May 1934 for the Moss Bank route and

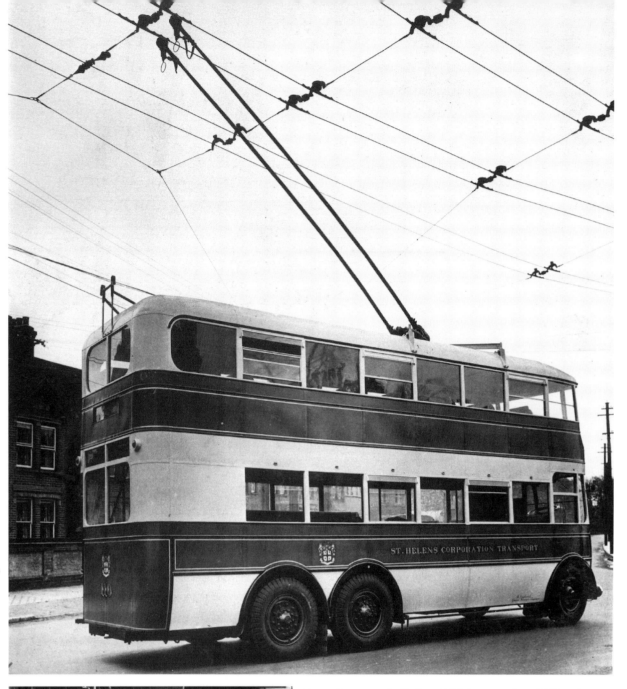

Above: Ransomes trolleybus 110 (later renumbered 115) undergoes tests in Ipswich before delivery. Note the vertical profile of the rear end, the absence of an upper-deck emergency door and of an offside cab door, a peculiarly St. Helens feature. The general manager's name, B. England, unusually appears on the offside.

Left: The 3-axle Ransomes trolleybuses of 1931 attracted the attention of the technical press when new as they were the first with a drop-frame at the rear of the chassis, facilitating a one-step platform. Number 111 undergoes a tilt test at Ransomes, Sims & Jeffries' works above what appears to be multi-gauge tramway track.

The policeman deals with the traffic outside the Town Hall as Brush-bodied Leyland TBD2 trolleybus 125 conveys a civic party, prior to the opening of the St. Helens-Nutgrove route in July 1934.

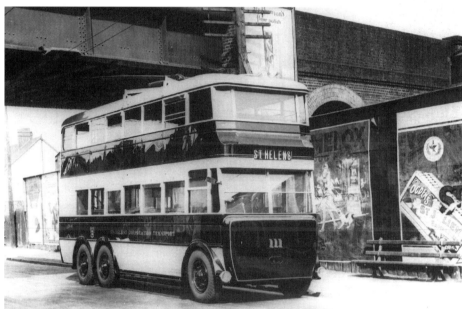

Ransomes trolleybus 111 on test in Ipswich before registration as DJ 4846. 'Transport' has replaced 'Tramways' in the title but the old-fashioned 'rocker panel' style of livery remains. The treatment of the front upper deck windows was unusual.

equipped with two front route indicators with the word 'VIA' permanently painted on the strip between them. They introduced a peculiar St. Helens feature, a double sliding window at the rear of the upper deck which doubled as an emergency exit and a means of access to the running gear on the roof. This was designed by manager A.A. Jackson who also had trolley wheels replaced by carbon skids except on the single-deckers and six-wheelers. These were sometimes changed in service using a small tower wagon, parts being passed through the rear sliding window to the operative on top.

In October 1942, an approach was made to Massey Bros. with a view to rebodying some trolleybuses which were suffering from premature body failure, apparently accelerated by being parked in the open at night during the air raid period. However, due to other commitments, Massey was unable to take on the work which went instead to East Lancashire Coachbuilders at Blackburn. Number 119 was selected to be done first and was fitted with a new East Lancs. body in November 1943. It received a GEC 80 hp motor, probably at the same time. It was the only one of its class to be rebodied, 116-8 being withdrawn in late 1945 and 120 in October 1948; 119 continued in service until December 1950. After withdrawal, both 116 and 118 acted as National Savings campaign buses and 118 became the post-war illuminated bus, the use of which was banned by the government because of the power shortage.

121-5 Chassis: Leyland TBD2   Body: Brush.
Motors: GEC WT254C 80 hp
series-wound, regulated field control.
Electrical equipment: GEC.

The bodies of these vehicles were identical to those of the previous batch. They were delivered in June and July 1934 for use on the through Prescot via Rainhill service. All were rebodied by East Lancashire at various dates between August 1945 and March 1947 and were withdrawn and scrapped in 1952.

Left: Awaiting departure for the Ram's Head, Haydock is Sunbeam W trolleybus 305 (DJ 9183), the first of a batch delivered in 1945 with 'relaxed utility' Roe bodies. The lowbridge design gave a very squat appearance, a feature shared with the Johannesburg wartime buses. Number 305 was withdrawn when the Atherton route was converted to motor bus operation on 30th November 1956.

Below left: Rebodied 1935 Leyland TBD2 trolleybus 129 waits to turn the corner from Cotham Street into Sefton Place. This was the last of sixteen trolleybuses to be rebodied by East Lancs. in November 1948 in an exercise spread over more than four years. The hackney carriage licence number over the wind-screen was an unusual feature on all trolleybuses licensed to ply for hire in St. Helens.

Above: This view of Sunbeam 377 and BUT 386 at the junction of New Road and Warrington Road, Rainhill clearly shows the distinctive rear emergency window, designed to facilitate ladder-access to the roof without breaking the glass, similar windows being fitted to some Cardiff vehicles. The famous skew railway bridge of 1829 is just out of the picture to the right.

Left: The ten Johannesburg trolleybuses retained the sharp front profile even after their rebuilding by Air Despatch/Bruce Coachworks, Cardiff. Number 358 is seen in Church Street working the peak hour 4A service to Boardman's Lane.

All the rebuilt Leyland TBD2s except 101-4 were withdrawn from service when the Moss Bank, Ackers Lane, Junction and Dentons Green routes were converted to motor bus operation on 3rd February 1952. Number 127 alone was stored in Jackson Street yard until sold for scrap later in the year.

This picture of 1935 Leyland TBD2 trolleybus 129 was used in Massey Bros. advertisements. Note the three-window arrangement at the front of the upper deck, designed to give additional support for the overhead gantry, and the permanent 'VIA' between the two front route indicators.

126-136 Chassis: Leyland TBD2   Body: Massey
Motors: GEC WT2511T 80 hp series-wound, regulated field control.
Electrical equipment: GEC.

These vehicles were similar in appearance to the previous deliveries but the bodies were built by Massey Bros. of Wigan. They were required for the St. Helens Junction and Dentons Green services, being delivered in May and June 1935. They were all rebodied by East Lancashire mostly between September 1944 and December 1945 though 135 was done in July 1946 and 129 as late as November 1948. All were withdrawn between January and September 1952.

137-144 Chassis: Ransomes D4   Body: Massey.
Motors: Ransomes 80 hp, Allen West control.
Electrical equipment: Crompton Parkinson.

Number 137-141 were placed in service for the conversion of the Prescot direct route in April 1936 and 142-4 in December 1936 and January 1937 to replace some of the single-deck fleet. Their Massey bodies were

of similar general layout and appearance as their predecessors. Numbers 137-8 and 141 had extensive body overhauls by Bankfield Engineering Co. of Southport in 1948. Their withdrawal was spread over 1949-52.

101-4 Chassis: Leyland TBD2   Body: Massey.
Motors: Metro-Vick MV201DW
80 hp series-wound, regulated-field control.
Electrical equipment: Metropolitan-Vickers.

Delivered in March 1937, these were of similar general layout to earlier vehicles. They were all rebodied by East Lancashire in 1947-48 and continued to run until November 1956, having been renumbered 301-4 in June 1955.

145-56 Chassis: Ransomes D4   Body: Massey.
Motors: Ransomes 80 hp (Allen West control)
Electrical equipment: Crompton Parkinson.

These vehicles, delivered between July and December 1938, were electrically identical to 137-44 but their bodies were of more modern appearance with a normal two-window front upper-deck arrangement. During

Rebodied 1937 Leyland 303 bound for Haydock, stands behind a 1930 South Lancs. Transport Guy in Sefton Place. The overhead linking the rest of the system with the Prescot circle, which was installed in 1949, can be seen top left.

Leyland TBD2 trolleybus 101, new in 1937, as rebodied by East Lancs. in 1948 is seen in Tolver Street workshop, adjoining Hall Street depot. As there were no wires, trolleybuses were towed into the workshops but returned to Hall Street by gravity. An RT is on an adjacent pit.

In earlier years, St. Helens Corporation borrowed Liverpool's illuminated tram for special occasions but in 1935, Garrett trolleybus No. 102 was decorated with coloured lights and was claimed as the first Illuminated trolleybus. It was used for a Hospital Carnival in 1935, the Coronation in 1937 and a further hospital fund-raising event in 1938. After the war, the Ministry of Fuel and Power forbade its use because of a power shortage and it was dismantled.

1948-49 all except 153 underwent extensive body overhauls – 146-7, 151-2 by Bankfield Engineering, Southport, 148-50, 154-5 by Marsden (Coachbuilders) Ltd., Warrington and 145 and 156 by an associate of East Lancs. which set up business in an aircraft hangar at Cardiff. Known originally as Air Despatch (Coachbuilders) Ltd., it was renamed Bruce Coachworks, Cardiff. The class was withdrawn between June 1950 and January 1952.

An unusual feature of all St. Helens trolleybuses except the last post-war deliveries was the absence of a cab door in the normal offside position; drivers reached the cab through a nearside door.

The Johannesburg Trolleybuses

During the 1939-45 war, a number of export orders for buses were diverted to the home market as there was no shipping available. There were at least two trolleybus

A battered Ransomes D4 trolleybus 153 (DJ 8128) squeezes past a Liverpool tram in St. Helens Road during the last month of tramway operation in Prescot. Note the sliding window in the rear emergency exit and the route number displayed in what had been the rear destination aperture. The tram stands on St. Helens-owned tracks for which Liverpool paid rent.

Ransomes trolleybus 150 came to grief after skidding on an icy patch on a journey from Moss Bank to Parr, only the concrete post on the left preventing it overturning. Note how the intermediate route indicator has been adapted for the route number.

orders for South Africa one of which was diverted to St. Helens. The chassis were 8ft wide and, as the maximum then permissible by British legislation was then 7ft 6in, special dispensation was given to operate them. There were 10 Sunbeam MF2 chassis powered by BTH 206E1 103 hp motors, electrical equipment also being by BTH. The motors were compound-wound with regenerative control and the feeders on the Prescot services had to be modified to deal with them.

These 10 vehicles (157-166), bodied by Massey, incorporated several 'utility' features but were not to the full Ministry of Supply austerity specification, having minimal upholstery. Despite their width, the standard three and four seating on the upper deck was retained. One feature was the provision of just one enormous front route indicator which displayed only numbers and this marked the start of route numbers in St. Helens. A side destination indicator was also provided. These vehicles were finished in all over grey and were used only on the Prescot circle until 1950 when 8 ft. wide vehicles became generally legal.

Like many wartime vehicles, the bodies contained much unseasoned wood and they required urgent attention at the end of the war. Massey Bros. agreed to renovate five but the first, submitted to them in March 1946 was not completed until May 1947 and they told the Corporation that, because of pressure on resources, they could do no more though two – 160 (after an accident) and 166, were eventually done by them. One (165) was done by East Lancs. Coachbuilders and Nos. 157-8, 161-3 went to Bruce Coachworks at Cardiff. The Corporation did two themselves, 159 and 164, the latter being completed in the new Tolver Street workshop and fitted with fluorescent lighting in 1948. Numbers 157-60, 162 and 164 were reseated in 1951-5 to 30/26. The whole batch were renumbered 357-66 in June 1955 and most were withdrawn in December 1955 though 361-2 survived until November 1956. All went for scrap.

The 'Wartime' Trolleybuses

Although they were always given the above name, these 10 vehicles were, in fact, delivered between September and December 1945, after the war had ended. Mounted on wartime Sunbeam W chassis, Nos. 105-114 had bodies by Charles H. Roe of Leeds built to the 'relaxed utility' specification. Although they had angular wartime

A top-deck interior view of Ransomes trolleybus No. 145, taken in wartime, shows the generally cramped accommodation, masked lights for the blackout the side gangway and the alternate rows of three and four seats.

The upper view shows the lowering of the negative wire in Warrington New Road. In the event of a highbridge bus attempting to go under the low bridge, the negative trolley boom would activate the microswitch shown in the lower view and cut off the power.

bodies, their seats were upholstered not the slatted wood of the full utility design. They had BTH 207A3 85 hp motors with compound-wound, stabilised rheostatic control. Number 112 was fitted with American-style trolley retrievers for some years in 1955-57. The experiment was not successful as the ropes tended to tangle with other high vehicles and no more were fitted.

They were renumbered 305-314 in June 1955 and most were withdrawn towards the end of 1956, 311 surviving until August 1957 and 312 until April 1958. All were scrapped.

The Highbridge Sunbeams and BUTs

Numbers. 174-189, the last trolleybuses to be purchased by St. Helens Corporation and the first to have highbridge bodies (15ft 2in overall) with normal two-and-two seating on the upper deck, comprised a split order, 174-181 being on Sunbeam F4 chassis and 182-9 on BUT 9611T chassis. BUT was a consortium formed to combine Leyland and AEC trolleybus manufacture. The Sunbeams had BTH 209 motors developing 95 hp at 550 volts or 103 hp at 600 volts; they had compound-wound stabilised rheostatic or contra-field control. The BUTs had English Electric 410B motors developing 120 hp at 550 volts with compound-wound, series dynamic control. The chassis had a short wheelbase to facilitate negotiating Thatto Heath railway bridge. They were the only St. Helens trolleybuses fitted with emergency traction batteries. Bodywork was by East Lancs. but the Sunbeams were made in the Bridlington factory with 55-seat bodies (29/26) while the BUTs were built at Blackburn with the more usual 30/26 seating. Apart from No. 164, they were the first St. Helens trolleybuses to have battery lighting instead of high tension current taken direct from the overhead line. They were 8 ft wide and equipped with compressed air operated screen-wipers and combined rheostatic and air brakes. Their fleet numbers were chosen to agree with registration numbers BDJ 74-89 and the numbers

167-173 were never used.

When delivered, they could not pass safely under Peasley Cross or Redgate bridges and were normally used only on the Prescot circle but, as a precaution, were fitted with a safety warning device designed in the department. The negative (nearside) wire at the approach to Peasley Cross bridge was divided in such a way that one boom was forced to one side and made contact with a switch on the roof which switched on a light, sounded a buzzer in the cab and cut off the power.

They were renumbered 374-389 in June 1955 and all survived until the trolleybus system closed on 30th June 1958. With the removal of some railway bridges, No. 380 was occasionally used on the Atherton service. Number 374 was the official last trolleybus on 1st July 1958. All were sold for further service elsewhere, the Sunbeams going to South Shields Corporation where they worked until 1963 and the BUTs to Bradford Corporation who withdrew them between March 1967 and June 1971, Numbers 383 and 387 being the last to run. Number 387 has been preserved and is fully restored to its St. Helens condition.

Leyland TBD2 No. 124 with Brush lowbridge bodywork was a typical example of the pre-war St. Helens trolleybus. Entering service in July 1934 for the Rainhill conversion, it received a new East. Lancs. body in October 1945 and continued in service until May 1952. Note the two-step platform, typical of trolleybuses of the period, and the long overhang of the trolley arms, necessary to deal with some of the bracket-arm overhead on the South Lancashire Transport system.

Operating Problems

As the trolleybus became extinct in St. Helens in 1958 and in Britain in 1972, some of its peculiar operating problems have been forgotten. On systems which operate abroad, technology has since advanced to enable trolleybuses to run through junctions at high speed but this was not the case before 1958 and one of the factors which influenced the replacement of trolleybuses by motor buses was the necessity of negotiating junctions at a speed not exceeding 5 mph with consequent delays to other traffic. Proceeding through a junction at high speed would almost invariably lead to dewirements with sometimes severe damage to the overhead. It is often forgotten that trolleybus overhead equipment is more than double the weight of tramway overhead as crossings of double wires require four times the amount of special work. Passing through a junction required the power to be switched off momentarily – another cause of delay – and operation of frogs (the points in the overhead line) required the power to be switched on or off when passing over the switch, depending on the direction required. In later years, it was the practice to divide the overhead line some distance before a junction so that the actual turn-out was actuated on a straight section.

In post-war years, staff difficulties led to a lowering of driving standards and it was necessary to issue frequent warnings to drivers following numerous

instances of careless driving resulting in dewirements, damage to the overhead and delays to the service. There was always a risk of a trolley head becoming detached with possibly fatal consequences if it struck a passer-by.

Power failures became more frequent in the immediate post-war years and the whole system would come to a standstill without warning. When power was restored, there was a risk of the line becoming overloaded if all the trolleybuses in a section switched on full power simultaneously, leading to a second failure. Drivers were instructed not to start from rest unless the trolleybus in front was at least three poles length (about 100 yd) ahead. In April 1949, staff were advised that the line voltage was being reduced because of power shortages between 7.30 and 9.0am and 4.30 and 6.30pm. This caused some current failures due to bunching and beyond the immediate environs of the town centre, drivers were instructed to keep at least 300 yd apart.

THE MOTOR BUS FLEET

In the summer of 1921, the Council accepted the tender of the Bristol Tramways and Carriage Co. Ltd. to supply buses and drivers for use during the relaying of certain sections of tramway. It seems likely that these buses were changed over during the hire which lasted until about the end of 1922. One of the buses, a Bristol 4-tonner with Bristol 32-seat body (HT 4367), new in December 1921, was painted red, the colour of the St. Helens trams. Another Bristol vehicle known to have been in St. Helens from 24th July to October 1921, was HT 4018, a 30-seater. At least three Hora-bodied AEC YC were hired from Liverpool Corporation during 1921.

The Council sanctioned the ordering of three buses, two Guy BA 20-seaters with Guy bodies and one Bristol 2-tonner with 24-seat Bristol body but the order for the latter was deferred and the Guys (Nos.2-3) arrived first in August-September 1923. The Bristol (No. 1) followed in January 1924. These buses carried a blue livery until 1925 when the Council decided to change to red and cream as used on the trams.

Two further Guy buses were purchased in 1924, another 20-seat BA with Guy body (4) and a BB with 32-seat rear-entrance Strachan and Brown body (5). Number 4 was rebodied by St. Helens Corporation in May 1930. Each of the next two years saw two further Guy BBs but with Guy dual-door 32-seat bodies supplied, 6-7 in 1925 and 8-9 in 1926. The latter pair eventually received new Corporation 32-seat bodies. These were all normal-control vehicles, i.e. with a bonnet, and the BBs must have been very cramped with 32 seats. Number 7 lost two seats in November 1932.

The acquisition of the St. Helens and District Motor Service Co. Ltd. on 1st June 1927 all but doubled the fleet overnight. Of the eight vehicles taken over, the oldest was a Daimler B, new in 1914, probably a charabanc when new, with a 26-seat Massey bus body. A Garner, with 20-seat unidentified body and two Daimler Y's, one with a 30-seat Massey body and the other with a 28-seat body of unknown origin, dated from 1921, though they carried registration numbers transferred from earlier vehicles. It seems likely that some of the bodies were newer than the chassis. A 1921 Daimler CK carried a 28-seat Northern Counties body. There followed three Leylands, a 1919 N (?) with a 32-seat Hora body, a 1925 C7 with 32-seat Northern Counties body and a 1926 C7 with 30-seat Leyland body. The N has also been described as having a Leyland body so the company probably indulged in the body-swapping which was common at the time. Its registration number (B 8841) may have belonged

This 1926 Leyland C7 was the last new bus to be purchased by the St. Helens & District Motor Service Co. Ltd. It carried the number 57 in their eight-bus fleet so that was probably the St. Helens licence number. It was numbered successively 16, 62 and 59 by the Corporation. It was reduced from 30 to 28 seats in November 1932 and fitted with a diesel engine in January 1933. This may have been experimental as it was rare for such an elderly vehicle to be so converted and the Corporation files record the fitting of a 'Leico' carburettor the same year. It was scrapped in December 1934.

Two Bristol B buses, with 32-seat bodies by the manufacturer, were supplied in June 1928 and numbered 17-18. J. Chorley, later Rolling Stock Superintendent, stands beside No. 18 which seems to have been regaled for some special occasion. The absence of a coat-of-arms is unusual. These buses, which had leather bucket seats, provided the service on the Parr route while trolleybus equipment was being installed.

originally to another vehicle. The company seems to have favoured Hora bodies as it is said to have taken delivery of its eighth Daimler with a Hora body in 1916. It is known that, in April 1921, it had enquired about the purchase of redundant Hora-bodied AECs from Liverpool Corporation though nothing came of that. These buses were numbered 10-17 in the municipal fleet. The company's numbers had been 3, 1, 6, 15, 21, 54, 57 and 20, suggesting that the municipal hackney carriage licences were used as fleet numbers.

One of the Daimler Y's (13) was rebodied with a 26-seat Corporation body almost immediately and the CK (12) was put on pneumatic tyres by August 1927; it received the Massey body from withdrawn Daimler B (11) in February 1931. The Garner (17) was renumbered 20 in May 1928 but almost immediately withdrawn for conversion into a municipal lorry in which role it served until 1936. Number 16 (by that time renumbered 62) was fitted with a diesel engine in January 1933. All the surviving vehicles had their seating capacities reduced in late 1932, probably to accord with the requirements of the Road Traffic Act, 1930.

Two Bristol B-type with Bristol 32-seat bodies (17-18) entered service in June 1928. They had bucket seats in red leather and were used initially on the new Warrington-Southport route. At the end of the year they were transferred to the Parr route pending the introduction of trolleybuses, being replaced on the Southport service by two Leyland PLSC3 Lions (19-20) with 32-seat Ransomes bodies. In March 1929 the whole fleet was renumbered – the first time of several – the principle being the allocation of Nos. 1-49 to the rapidly dwindling tram fleet, 50-100 to motor buses and 101-up to trolleybuses. Numbers 1-9 became 50-58; 10-12 became 67, 69, 68; 13-20 became 59-66.

The First Double Deck Buses

The 20-strong fleet remained adequate for over two years and the next additions were the Corporation's first four double-deckers, all-Leyland Titan TD1s with 48-seat lowbridge bodies (69-72),the upper decks having alternate rows of three and four seats to assist circulation; they were the last new petrol-engined buses to enter the fleet. They replaced the two Daimler Ys and the Leyland N (59-60, 67) the numbers of which were taken in July 1932 by three all-Crossley Condor lowbridge double-

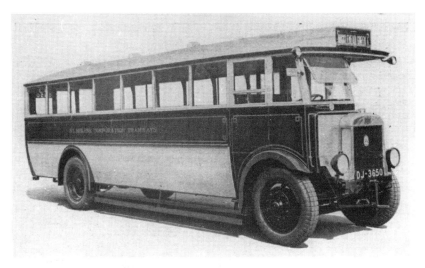

The two Leyland PLSC3 Lions delivered in August 1928 present an unusual appearance as their Ransomes bodies were more deeply skirted than the much more common Leyland product. Number 19 is showing the destination for the Sunday service between Toll Bar and Micklehead Green. Both had ten-year lives in St. Helens and then went to showmen.

St. Helens was an early convert to diesel propulsion and three TD2s, (76-8), delivered in May 1933, were fitted with the original Leyland 8.1-litre E28 engine. Note the additional beading strips to divide the red and cream on the lower panels and the route boards which were short-lived. Number 76 was withdrawn from service in December 1947 becoming a departmental lorry.

deck buses, originally fitted with Crossley diesel engines but these were replaced by Leyland engines in 1936. The 48-seat Crossley bodies were, except in matters of detail, identical to those used extensively in Manchester. They were renumbered 73-75 in March 1934. Only lowbridge buses were acquired for many years because of the danger posed by the low railway bridge near Peasley Cross.

Three all-Leyland Titan TD2 lowbridge buses, delivered in May 1933, were the first diesel-engined vehicles to enter the fleet, being fitted with the original Leyland E28 8.1-litre engine. They had brackets for route boards fitted below the upper deck windows. This was a short-lived policy applied also to a few trolleybuses.

The next acquisitions were three secondhand 1927 Bristol B buses with 32-seat Northern Counties bodies from Wigan Corporation where they had been Nos. 21, 23 and 30. In St. Helens they were initially numbered 73-75 but were renumbered 60-62 after only a few months. This necessitated 61-62 (formerly 15-16) being renumbered 58-59, numbers which they carried for only a few months until their withdrawal. Also withdrawn in 1933 were the original Bristol 2-tonner (50) and three Guys (55, 56, 58).

Leyland Standardisation

The 1934 intake, and all subsequent deliveries up to the outbreak of war, were fitted with Leyland hydraulic torque converters (so-called 'Gearless Buses'). They comprised five Leyland Tiger TS6c's with 32-seat English Electric bodies (51-54). Four more (56-59) came in 1935 plus another four with Leyland bodies (60-61, 67-68). They were equipped with twin front route indicator boxes with the word 'VIA' painted between them and a single line box at the rear and nearside. This layout remained standard for both single- and double-deck buses in the pre-war years. Two Guys (51/3) were briefly renumbered 58, 56 to accommodate them. All the remaining Guys and ex-St. Helens District vehicles were cleared out in 1934.

Five Leyland Tiger TS6c buses (51-5) with 32-seat English Electric bodies entered service in June 1934, followed by a second batch of four in December (56-59). They introduced the two line destination indicator layout with 'VIA' permanently painted between the two. Number 51 is showing 'via Newton and Leigh', designed for display on the Liverpool-Manchester service but St. Helens buses never actually participated. They were all converted to perimeter seating during the war, allowing 30 standing passengers and several were rebodied after the war.

There were no new buses in 1936 but 1937 saw the delivery of six all-Leyland TS8c 32-seat saloons (62-66, 79) followed by four more the following year (80-84). There were also four all-Leyland TD5c 50-seat double-deckers (85-88). The Bristol Bs and PLSC3 Lions (63-66) briefly carried Nos. 83-86 before withdrawal in 1937-38. The final 'pre-war' intake comprised four all-Leyland TD7c double-deckers (69-72) which did not arrive until December 1939, the TD1s (69-72) being renumbered 89-92 though 89-90 were withdrawn in June 1940, the latter going to Leigh Corporation for spares. A further TD7, but fitted with a gearbox, was allocated under the government's 'unfrozen' scheme, having been part of an order placed by the Scottish Motor Traction Co. This had a Leyland 53-seat body, all the upper deck seats except the rear one being in rows of four. This arrived in May 1942 and took the now vacant number 89.

Wartime Buses

Additional factory services during the war resulted in the Corporation being allocated eight Guy Arab buses with lowbridge double-deck utility bodies. These had solid rear emergency windows and only two opening windows each side, as specified by the Ministry of Supply. They were powered by 7-litre Gardner 5LW 5-cylinder engines. The bodies were built at Wigan by Northern Counties. Because of local weight restrictions, the Mk I Arabs (93-97) seated 24/26 and the Mk II Arabs (98-100) seated 27/26 whereas the standard utility arrangement was 27/28. Delivery was spread from September 1942 to November 1943. The Mk II buses had the longer bonnet designed to accommodate the more powerful 8.4-litre 6LW engine but they were 5LW-powered on delivery. Two further models of this type, numbered 75, 90 were delivered in February-

March 1945, with bodies by Weymann, this time with the normal 27/28 seating arrangement. All the utility buses were painted grey on delivery.

Numbers 97-100 were delivered with slatted wooden seats but 93-96 had seats with minimum upholstery as fitted to the Johannesburg trolleybuses. The wooden seats were replaced by upholstered seats from withdrawn TD1 and TD2 buses in 1947-48, seating being reduced to 50 because of bridge weight restrictions; 96 and 97 were extensively overhauled by Bruce Coachworks at Cardiff. Number 100 was rebuilt by the Corporation in 1949, with a 6LW engine and novel upper-deck quarter-lights. All the utility buses except 98-99 had sliding windows fitted on both decks after the war and route number boxes (except 94 and 99). The rear emergency doors were glazed and all were repainted in the current livery.

As several colliery services were restricted to single-deck buses by low bridges, the capacity of the nine English Electric-bodied Leyland TS6c's (51-9) was increased by rearranging their seats round the perimeter of the saloon and authorising additional standing passengers for whom extra grab rails were fitted.

The fleet was further augmented during the war by two Leyland TD4c's with Massey 52-seat highbridge bodies, hired from Bolton Corporation who had surplus

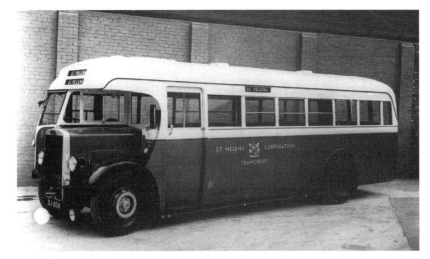

St. Helens continued to favour the Leyland metal-framed body which was not universally acclaimed and specified it for six TS8c 32-seaters in 1937 (62-66, 79) and a further four (80-84) in 1938. There were slight variations in the body styling, including the placing of the side destination indicator in the cantrail instead of in a box hanging in a window. However, the new livery with much more pale cream, imparted a much brighter effect. All had their torque-convertors replaced by gearboxes in 1946-48. Number 81 was renumbered 247 in 1948 and sold for further service in 1952.

Leyland TS6c 54 was the first of its kind to be refurbished by the Corporation after the war and retained its front canopy, all the others dealt with having half canopies. New big destination indicators and route numbers were fitted and the vehicle is shown on 'the land' outside the depot in company with Guy Arab 97, the last to have slatted wooden seats and to run in grey wartime livery.

buses, having received buses for tramway replacements which were deferred or reversed. They retained their Bolton fleet numbers 31 and 37 and were the only highbridge buses to run in St. Helens during that era.

1946-50

Fleet renewal in the immediate post-war years was a slow process as every operator had years of arrears to overcome and the manufacturers simply could not keep pace with the flood of orders. Bureaucratic interference, skill and material shortages and labour unrest all added to the problems. In addition there was a tremendous pent-up demand for travel so that many operators needed to augment their fleets substantially. The combined trolley- and motor bus fleets of St. Helens Corporation had increased from 94 to 111 during the war period, an increase of 18% but more in terms of seats as the proportion of double-deck buses had grown.

Two buses caught fire during 1945, allegedly because paraffin had leaked from their torque-converters. One was 71 which was extensively reconditioned by East Lancs. in December of that year. Every user was experiencing difficulty in maintaining that equipment which was now out of production. St. Helens adopted a policy of fitting orthodox gearboxes as soon as it could obtain them, commencing with the 1938-39 buses in 1946 and working back to the earlier models by 1950.

New buses for 1946 comprised four Bristol K6A with Strachan lowbridge bodies built to the 'relaxed' utility standards with upholstered seats and normal opening windows. One, which became No. 48, was to the post-war design with the engine and radiator mounted lower in the chassis frame. They introduced a new route indicator layout which was to be standard for the next few years, consisting of a single-line destination with a three-column route number alongside but offset slightly to the off-side so that the number blinds were directly over the driver's cab. A destination box was mounted over the saloon window nearest the door. As motor bus fleet numbers had already reached 100, they were numbered downwards from 50 to 47 and this policy was continued until 1949. However a separate series was created for second-hand or hired vehicles. Three Leyland TD1s and a TD2, dating from 1930-33 were bought from Wigan Corporation for £250 each in December 1946, becoming 17-20.

Hired Vehicles

Meanwhile, a 1935 TS6c (59), which had been involved in a serious accident in August 1945, was converted to a TD3 double-decker with a new East Lancs. lowbridge body in July 1946 but with no more new vehicles in sight, six single-deck vehicles had to be hired to enable improved services to be brought in at the end of September

The final four Leyland TS6c saloons had Leyland 32-seat metal-framed bodies, entering service in the summer of 1935. The header tank for the torque convertor is clearly visible in the upper view. Note the rear destination indicator, unusual in this type of body. Number 60 became 251 in 1948, received a new Roe body in 1950 and ran until 1954 – a 19 year life.

1946. These were three 1928-29 Tilling Stevens B10A from Western National Omnibus Co. Ltd. but new to North Western. They had 32-seat Mumford coach bodies and cost £1.7.6d (£1.37½) per day; one 1928 Bristol B with a 31-seat centre-entrance Roe body from Rotherham Corporation at £17.10.0d per month and two 1932 Dennis Lancets with 26-seat Grose bodies from Northampton Corporation at £20 per month each. These buses were numbered between 21 and 26 in the St. Helens fleet. The three Tilling Stevens were returned in March-April 1947 and the Bristol in June, being replaced by two 1929 Leyland Lion LT1s with 31-seat Roe dual-entrance bodies from Bury Corporation at £15 per month each plus tyres and licences and two 1931 LT3 Lions from Leigh Corporation at £20 per month each. The former retained their own fleet numbers 14-15 while the latter became 27-28. The last hired vehicles, the Northampton Lancets and Leigh Lions, went back in July to September 1948.

Slow Deliveries

The delays in deliveries of new vehicles was extremely frustrating to transport managers anxious to upgrade their fleets and improve services to the public. There was an imbalance of capacity between chassis and body manufacturers as the latter were dealing with refurbishment orders as well as bodies for new vehicles. In St. Helens, new deliveries had done little more than keep up with withdrawals, all the Crossley and Leyland TD2 double-deck buses of 1932-33 being withdrawn during 1947, TD2 No. 78 having been completely destroyed by fire.

Six AEC Regent II chassis, ordered in April 1946, were delivered relatively quickly as the Regent II was an updated version of the pre-war Regent I, using mainly

Four Bristol K6A with Strachan bodies to relaxed utility standards (47-50), delivered in 1946, were the first new buses to carry the new standard destination indicator layout with route numbers slightly offset to the off-side, to simplify driver control. This view of No. 48 was used as an advertisement by Bristol.

Guy Arab 100, new in 1943 as a 5LW with Northern Counties utility body, was rebuilt in 1949 as a 6LW by the Corporation. New indicators and sliding windows were fitted and wooden seats replaced but the most striking features were the upper-deck roof lights, designed to dispel the gloom of the lowbridge style top deck. It remained in service until 1956, the last of the wartime Guys.

Leyland TD1 No. 19, new in December 1930, was one of four Wigan Corporation buses (17-20) bought for £250 each in December 1946. This one was rebuilt only to the extent of having new destination equipment fitted to the piano front. Withdrawn from service in July 1950, Nos. 17 and 19 were used as snowploughs for another seven years and 19 is shown, connected to the radiator heating equipment in Jackson Street open-air parking ground in 1953.

parts which had been manufactured in the early war years and stored. These were the first buses of this make to be ordered by St. Helens Corporation. When the chassis arrived, they had to be stored because East Lancs. Coachbuilders was too busy to take them and the buses finally entered service in June 1948, two years and two months after the order was placed. Of seven bodybuilders invited to tender, East Lancs. was the only one to bid for the supply of eight bodies to be mounted on Bristol L single-deck chassis. In November 1947, 16 months after the order was placed and several months after the chassis had been delivered to their works at Blackburn, East Lancs. asked to be released from their contract, suggesting that Charles H. Roe might be in a position to take it over. At first it was proposed that Roe should body four of them but eventually all eight were completed at their Leeds works.

The following table illustrates the delivery delays experienced at this time.

Particulars of Order	Date	Date Delivered	Total Time
7 DD (Ministry of Supply Order)	May 1945	Feb-Mar 1946 (4) July 1947 (3)	9-10 months 2yr 2 mths
3 Leyland PD1	Feb. 1946	Sep. 1947	1yr 7 mths
6 AEC Regent II	Apr. 1946	June 1948	2yr 2 mths
8 Bristol L6A	July 1946	Sep. 1948	2yr 2 mths
8 AEC Regent III	July 1946	Oct. 1949	3yr 2 mths
8 trolleybuses	July 1946	Dec. 1950	4yr 5 mths

The three Bristol K6As (44-46) and three Leyland PD1s (41-43) delivered in 1947, six AEC Regent IIs (35-40) in 1948 and eight AEC Regent IIIs (27-34) in 1949 all received the same style of lowbridge East

Lancs. body but the AECs lacked radiused lower saloon windows. The Roe bodies fitted to the eight Bristol L6A single-deck buses had rear-entrances and seated 35. They introduced a further variation to the fleet numbering system whereby single-deck motor buses were numbered from 201 up. In March 1948 all earlier single-deck buses were renumbered between 240 and 262 in a somewhat haphazard manner and this gave sufficient flexibility in the numbering scheme to avoid repeating the frequent renumberings of the past.

The Reconditioning Programme

In view of the non-availability of sufficient new vehicles, the Corporation embarked on a refurbishment programme which, including trolleybuses, involved 65 vehicles. As the need coincided with alterations to the depot and workshops, most of this work had to be sent out. Each vehicle was assessed and the necessary work carried out, ranging from new bodies, through major reconstruction to repanelling. With post-war inflation, some of the major rebuilds cost more than the new bodies. All vehicles had the post-war standard destination equipment fitted during their refurbishment.

Six 1934-35 TS6s were rebodied by Roe, three with 36-seat rear entrance and three as 33-seat dual entrance bodies in 1949-50; four others and a TS8c had major body overhauls. Four pre-war Leyland double-deckers and two Guys received similar treatment. Five other vehicles had some attention while undergoing accident repairs which were contracted out. Three of the ex-Wigan TD1s were extensively rebuilt between October 1948 and February 1949, No. 17 having £1,380 spent on

AEC RT No. 12 was one of the second batch (Nos. 1-25) and entered service in January 1952. It was built to full London Transport specification and was photographed while still in original condition when on a private hire in Manchester in May 1953. These buses were low enough to pass under Peasley Cross bridge and a selection of appropriate route numbers was provided on the single blind used in London as an intermediate blind. This bus was renumbered 32 in October 1961 and was one of the last RTs to be withdrawn in February 1962, passing to Hunt of Bickerstaffe.

Because of the restricted width of Woodlands Road, where two 8ft buses could not pass, St. Helens Corporation used 7ft 6in wide buses on the Carr Mill No. 55 service and Nos. 83-91 were Leyland PD2/22, 27ft long and 14ft 3½in high but with narrow 58-seat bodies by East Lancs. They were the first St. Helens buses with heaters and, following in the RT tradition, they had rear wheel discs and could be used on most routes. After withdrawal in 1967, No. 83 saw further service with Paton Bros. Ltd. of Renfrew. Note that RT No. 24 behind had had its route number indicator modified to the more economical three-column layout.

In 1962 it was still quite rare for a municipal operator to have a new coach. Number 200, a Leyland Leopard L2 had been a Duple demonstrator at the 1962 Commercial Motor Show. With full air suspension, its 41-seat body was of the Britannia style. It was sold to a dealer in 1971.

it, about 70% of the cost of a new body. Despite this, they were all withdrawn in July 1950, 20, which was not rebuilt, having already gone in October 1949.

The three dual entrance buses, 251/3-4 were used on a passenger flow experiment from August 1950, the hand-operated rear door being used as an entrance and the electrically-operated front door as an exit. Conductors were told to enforce this strictly. After about three months, a 'purdah' glass window was fitted behind the driver's cab to obviate the need for a blind at night and the door controls were duplicated to enable either driver or conductor to operate them. The experiment was

obviously unsuccessful as, in February 1951, staff were instructed to use the rear door only. Single-deck requirements were declining and eight were declared redundant in September 1951.

There had even been a proposal to return to service a Bristol B bus manufactured in 1927 which St. Helens had bought second-hand from Wigan Corporation in 1933. This was former No. 75 (later 82) which had been withdrawn in 1937 and converted into a Gas Testing Chamber for the Air Raid Precautions people. The police returned it to the Transport department in August 1946 without engine, transmission or seats and with the

This design of four-bay lowbridge body by East Lancs. was representative of the St. Helens buses of the late 1940s and was mounted successively on Bristol K6A, Leyland PD1 and AEC Regent II and III chassis as shown in these three photographs. The 1947 style on the Bristols and Leylands had radiused lower-deck saloon windows but this was not repeated on the 1948-49 AECs.

windows boarded up. A second-hand engine, clutch and gearbox were bought for £200 and the vehicle was placed over a pit while a fruitless search was made for other obsolete Bristol spare parts but eventually the quest was abandoned as hopeless and the remains were scrapped.

The immediate post-war Bristol and Leyland double-deck buses had long lives, being withdrawn in September 1959 and July 1960 respectively. The AECs were sold in 1957-59. The eight single-deck Bristols were originally employed on the Warrington-Southport route which was restricted by the low bridge at Rainford until 1952. However, they were found other work; No. 204 became a mobile Co-op shop in 1955, 207-8 were withdrawn at the end of 1956, 201-3 and 205 in 1963 and the last survivor, 206 in December 1964.

Standardisation

The division of orders between AEC, Bristol and Leyland had been an expedient to get as many new buses as quickly as possible but by 1948, AEC was the preferred make. The Bristols were AEC powered but, following the nationalisation of the Bristol company, the marque could not be sold outside the nationalised Groups. R. Edgeley Cox, who became general manager in 1949, had been involved with the development of the London Transport RT type and persuaded the Committee that this was the ideal vehicle for St. Helens despite its higher cost. The comparative figures were – for the standard Regent III chassis £1,806-13-3d plus body £2155, total £3,961; for RT chassis £2,030, body £2,395 total £4,425. The special advantage of the RT in St. Helens was that its height of 14ft 3½ in enabled it to pass safely under both Peasley Cross and Ellamsbridge Road bridges and its adoption would reduce the number of lowbridge buses. Furthermore, the RT chassis were immediately available, possibly because of some special influence possessed by Mr Cox.

An order was placed for 15 RTs with 56-seat Park Royal bodywork to full London specification which arrived in May to July 1950. They were numbered 59-73 and made such an impression that a second order was placed for 25 (1-25) which were delivered between December 1951 and February 1952. All 40 had the full London destination blind equipment but St. Helens used the large intermediate blind, front and rear, to display the route number, the smaller aperture being used for a rather cramped intermediate route display. The side blind over the entrance was partially masked to show the destination only. At first a single route number roll was employed but this was eventually replaced by three separate rolls. St. Helens was the only provincial fleet to buy London-type RTs new with full London destination equipment.

The first underfloor-engined vehicle was placed in service on the Warrington-Southport service on 25th February 1951. This was an AEC Regal IV (209) with Roe 42-seat dual-entrance body. More were to have been ordered but the replacement of the low bridge at Rainford enabled this long route to be worked by double-deckers.

In 1952, Mr Cox left to take over as general manager at Walsall where he was instrumental in extending the trolleybus system; his replacement was Mr J.C. Wake, an accountant by training, who placed much more stress on the financial aspects of management decisions. There were no more expensive RTs but the policy of reduced height double-deck bodies was continued,

AEC Regal IV No. 209 with dual-door 42-seat Roe body was the first underfloor engined vehicle in the fleet. It entered service in February 1951 and was intended for use on the long Warrington-Southport route which was then restricted by the low bridge at Rainford. More were to have been ordered but the replacement of the bridge made this unnecessary and 209 remained unique for several years. It was sold in 1965, seeing brief further service with Grayshott Coaches in Hampshire.

bodybuilders being persuaded to modify their standard designs to keep the overall height down to 14ft 3½in. Mr Wake also introduced a system of prefix letters to indicate, retrospectively, the Council sanction for the purchase of particular batches of vehicles. From an operational point of view, they gave guidance as to the allocation of buses to duties as the highest lettered buses were naturally preferred for all day duties. All earlier double-deck buses received prefixes but not single-deckers. The surviving wartime buses had an 'A' prefix.

The first prefixed buses were nine Leyland Titan PD2/9 double-deckers with 56-seat bodies by Davies of Merthyr, delivered in 1954 and numbered E74-82. They were followed later the same year by nine PD2/22s with 58-seat East Lancs. bodywork (E83-91). These buses were the first to have heaters and were unusual in being to the new 27ft length but only 7ft 6in wide, 'narrow' buses being required for the Carr Mill via Woodlands Road service where, on one section, 8ft wide buses could not pass. Four of the PD2/9s were retained

beyond their normal lifespan until July 1968 to work this route. The PD2/9s were in fact the only vehicles of this designation to be built; they had the traditional exposed radiator but the PD2/22s were the first to sport the so-called 'tin-front'. The 1955 deliveries comprised nine PD2/20s with 61-seat 8ft wide East Lancs. bodies (F101-9) of similar general appearance to E83-91.

The Corporation thought Davies bodies were good value for money and ordered 11 more to be mounted on Leyland PD2/20 chassis for delivery in 1956. However, only one was delivered as the business was closed down following the death of the owner and the balance of the order was transferred elsewhere. Between November 1956 and January 1957 24 PD2/20s entered service, 13 with Weymann bodies (F110-1, 113-7, G128-33), 10 with East. Lancs. (G118-27) and one by Davies (F112). All had the now standard configuration of 33 seats over 28 with reduced height. Six Weymann-bodied AEC Regent Vs followed in August 1957 (H134-9). The AEC marque was once more in favour and a further 24

Number 59, the first of 15 AEC RTs to full London specification is handed over to St. Helens Corporation by Park Royal Vehicles in May 1950. Mr R. Edgeley Cox, general manager is shown (far left) next to Councillor Walter Marshall, chairman of the Transport Committee, with AEC and Park Royal officials. The bus was used for driver familiarisation before entering service in June.

The Leyland-bodied Leyland TS8s required less attention than the English Electrics but 64 (242) and 82 (248) were rebuilt in this style with one large destination indicator instead of two small ones but no route numbers. Number 242 shown here was refurbished by Bankfield Engineering at Southport at a cost of £507. Note the cutaway rear end to avoid fouling hump-backed bridges.

The 7ft 6in wide Davies bodies bore a superficial resemblance to the Park Royal bodies on the RTs. Numbers 74-82 were the only Leyland PD2/9 models to be built. New in 1954, No. 80 was withdrawn in 1965 and, with three others of its class, saw further service with Barton Transport.

entered service in 1958, 16 with Weymann bodies (J140-55) and eight with East. Lancs. bodies (J156-63). In 1959, the seating plan was modified to 36 over 28, eight Weymann-bodied Regent Vs (K164-71) being the first to have this arrangement. The earlier Regent Vs were powered by the AEC AV370 7.68-litre engine but from J140, the A218 9.6-litre engine was fitted.

In 1958, the general manager had asked for authority to purchase two forward-entrance high-capacity double-deck buses. One, a 30ft-long Regent V with East Lancs 73-seat body (K199) arrived in December 1959 but, at that stage, Leyland was unable to produce a 14ft 3°in Atlantean so that order was cancelled. K199 remained as the only 30ft double-deck bus in the fleet and the only forward entrance bus. It was a jinxed bus and once blew its engine on the M6 when returning from Blackburn on a private hire, bits being scattered along the inside lane, but its main problem was that the fuel tank was too small to enable it to run all day on the Warrington-Southport service; it ran out of fuel more than once on the 22.20 from Southport, always way out in the country. In 1964, the manager, by then A.C. Barlow, recommended that

no more large capacity double-deck buses be purchased as the initial cost and fuel consumption were higher and he was opposed to making economies by running larger buses on reduced frequencies.

The first RTs were withdrawn in August 1960, the second batch (D1-25) going first to avoid spending money on preparation for certification; they were followed by the earlier buses in 1962. Many saw further service with other operators, notably Hull Corporation (19) and Harper Bros. (Heath Hayes) Ltd. (7).

The fleet now totalled around 140 vehicles and remained at this level for a decade. Eight Leyland PD2/30s (K172-9) which came in 1960 had the body order split equally between Weymann and East Lancs. The standard 36 over 28 seating arrangement was retained on this and all but the final subsequent double-deck orders. The following two years' order was divided between AEC and Leyland. The former provided seven Regent Vs (L1-7) in 1961 and eight (L33-40) in 1962 all with Metropolitan-Cammell Orion-style bodies with single-line front destination indicators and numbers only at the side and rear. Leyland supplied 25 PD2A/30s, 12 bodied by East Lancs. (L8-12 in 1961 and L26-32 in 1962) and 13 with Metropolitan-Cammell Orion-style bodies (L13-25). The 'A' suffix in the type indicated a fibreglass bonnet front, a variant available on PD2 and PD3 models from 1960. St. Helens commissioned an unusual assymmetrical front which was subsequently used elsewhere and known as the 'St. Helens front'. Two RTs (D11-2) were renumbered D31-2 for their last four months' service.

The Corporation also purchased its first coach in 1962, a Leyland Leopard L2 (200) with full air suspension and 41-seat centre-entrance Duple Britannia body which had been exhibited at the 1962 Commercial Motor Show. Most of the 1962 vehicles were eventually

transferred to Merseyside though four, withdrawn in December 1973 and early 1974, went to Canada where they were still operating for Vancouver Island Coach Lines Ltd. (Gray Line Tours) ten years later. The coach was sold in 1971 being replaced by a second-hand 1968 diesel-engined Bedford VAM70 (201) with 45-seat centre-entrance Duple body, originally with N. Boyes of Bradford.

With the fall in traffic and likelihood of a change to one-man operation, there was now, once more, a need for new single-deck vehicles in the fleet and three AEC Reliance underfloor-engined buses with 45-seat front-entrance bodies by Marshall of Cambridge (210-2) were taken into stock in April 1963 and a further two similar vehicles in February 1965 (213-4). These were rebuilt as 41-seat one-man buses in November 1966. However the double-deck fleet received a further nine PD2A/30s in 1965, five by East Lancs. (L41-5) and four with Metropolitan-Cammell Orion-style bodies (L46-9). These were the last buses to have prefixed fleet numbers. The Corporation's 1967 and last double-deck order before adopting a single-deck standee vehicle policy was again split between AEC and Leyland. Three Regent Vs (56-8) had Metropolitan-Cammell bodies and six PD2A/27s (50-5) had East Lancs. bodywork. All nine had 37 upper deck seats instead of 36 as hitherto. The adoption of the PD2A/27 variant of the Titan signalled a change of policy from vacuum- to air-brakes.

When the St. Helens undertaking was acquired by Merseyside PTE on 1st April 1974, a number of ex-Birkenhead Corporation Leyland PD2/40s were transferred to St. Helens. Surprisingly, they were all painted in St. Helens-style livery with a 'Merseyside' fleet name in a small box which subsequently gave way to the more familiar 'Catherine wheel' logo. Ex-Birkenhead 113 was a 1965 vehicle with 66-seat Massey bodywork. Initially numbered 30, it then became 60W. An accident with an AEC Swift demolished the rear end and it served in the driving school from 1977 to 1981. It became a towing vehicle, eventually passing to Merseybus and has been preserved.

Buses parked between peaks on 'the land' opposite Hall Street depot. Left to right are 1963 AEC Reliance 210 one of the first three 45-seat Marshall bodied vehicles in the fleet; the solitary high capacity double-decker, AEC Regent V 199 with 73-seat East Lancs. body; Leyland PD2/20 122 with 1956 East Lancs. body and 1962 AEC Regent V 35 with 64-seat Metro-Cammell bodywork.

The standard one-man vehicle in St. Helens was the AEC Swift with Marshall dual-entrance 44-seat body. No fewer than 63 were purchased by the Corporation between 1968 and 1973; three were bought second-hand from Lancashire United and a further nine, ordered by the Corporation, were delivered to the PTE in 1975 - a grand total of 75. No. 245 is shown outside Hall Street depot after delivery in 1971, having been delayed because of London Transport orders. Note the perpetuation of the rear wheel trims, more than 20 years after the first RTs went into service.

The AEC Swift Fleet

For its one-man operation programme, St. Helens Corporation standardised on the AEC Swift with 44-seat dual-entrance Marshall body, licensed to carry 20 standing passengers. Eighteen were delivered in 1968 entering service on the Carr Mill and Prescot Circle services. They were followed by nine in 1969, 18 in 1971, nine in 1972 and nine in 1973, the latter with 42-seat bodies. Fleet numbers ran from 215 to 277. A further three 1969 Swifts (291-3) were bought second-hand from Lancashire United Transport Ltd. in 1973; these had 43-seat dual-entrance Alexander bodies and retained the fleet numbers carried in the LUT fleet. A further nine Marshall-bodied Swifts (278-86), ordered by St. Helens Corporation, were delivered to Merseyside PTE in 1975.

Vehicle Transfers

As the day for the transfer of the St. Helens transport undertaking to Merseyside Passenger Transport Executive approached, fleet requirements were considered in conjunction with the PTE. The withdrawal of time-expired double-deckers left the undertaking short of this type and the PTE organised the transfer of three 1956-7 Leyland PD2/20s with 60-seat Weymann Aurora bodies to St. Helens from Southport Corporation whose undertaking was also to be acquired from 1st April 1974. The liveries were very similar and these buses had 100 added to their Southport fleet numbers, becoming 131, 134 and 137. A further vehicle from the same batch, 135, was transferred in the first month of PTE management. One of Southport's 11 m Leyland

Nationals (2), a 46-seat dual door bus, worked in St. Helens in February and March 1974 and a Northern Counties bodied 43-seat dual-door AEC Swift of Nottingham Corporation was demonstrated in January 1974.

Also transferred in April-May were four 1965-6 Massey-bodied Leyland PD2/40s, new to Birkenhead Corporation whose fleet had been absorbed by the PTE on formation in 1969. Before transfer, they were repainted in the St. Helens colours of red and cream and initially took fleet numbers 30-33. A further seven ex-Birkenhead PD2/40s, dating from 1963, were transferred to St. Helens between June and September 1974 and numbered 34-40. However, all the Birkenhead buses were renumbered 60-70W in September 1974, the W apparently indicating the PTE's Wirral division. A twelfth bus which had been transferred to Liverpool earlier and renumbered L370 in the ex-Liverpool series came to St. Helens in September 1974 but was passed on to Southport, together with 70W, in December 1974.

The total St. Helens fleet transferred to the PTE comprised 127 vehicles as follows:-

23	AEC Regent V
2	AEC Reliance
66	AEC Swift
1	Bedford VAM70
3	Leyland PD2/20 (ex Southport)
6	Leyland PD2A/27
26	Leyland PD2A/30
127	TOTAL

The PTE pursued a policy of maximising the use of the fleet communally and, as the AEC Regent Vs were compatible with the ex-Liverpool fleet, eight of them (1, 2, 4, 33-35, 147 and 155) were transferred to Liverpool at various dates between July 1974 and July 1975 and were given Liverpool green livery and fleet numbers A454-61 (not in order). They were used on low-mileage peak hour duties, five surviving until January 1977 when crew operation ended in Liverpool.

The PTE also took the Bedford coach away, repainted it green and cream and renumbered it C201; it was used for private hire and finally withdrawn in August 1981.

From October 1974, the PTE abandoned its policy of retaining constituent liveries and all subsequent vehicles were painted in a standard livery described as verona green and buttermilk. The last bus to carry St. Helens red livery was No. 44 which was never repainted.

Upper: St. Helens Corporation's only experiment with high-capacity double-deckers, AEC Regent V No. 199, spent its first two years on the Prescot Circle (7/8) and Eccleston-Parr (15/16) routes because of a dispute about standing passengers. After this was settled it often worked to Southport. It is seen at Warrington (Arpley) bus station on the 9.15am Southport departure on a Sunday, the only St. Helens-worked journey to show 309 as the Corporation normally worked the 319 trips via Barrow Nook. In fact this trip was a feeder, through passengers being transferred to a Ribble bus at St. Helens.

Centre: Lancashire United Transport sold their three 1969 AEC Swifts with 43-seat dual-entrance Alexander bodies to St. Helens Corporation in 1973. They retained their LUT fleet numbers 291-3 and No. 292 is seen loading for Prescot via Rainhill outside the old market in Bridge Street.

Lower: Number 56 was one of the last three double-deck buses purchased by St. Helens Corporation, entering service on 1st July 1967. They were AEC Regent V chassis, powered by AV590-9.6-litre engines and had Metro-Cammell Orion-type bodies seating 65 passengers. It is seen by the Co-op in Baldwin Street showing both destinations of service 6, an ex-trolleybus route. It remained in PTE service until 1980.

ST. HELENS TRAM FLEET

STEAM TRAMWAYS

LOCOMOTIVES

Fleet No.	Manufacturer	Type	Date in Service	Date Withdrawn	Remarks
1-6	Thos.Green & Son Ltd.	HP cyl. 9" dia.14" stroke LP cyl. 14" dia.14" stroke	1-2/1890	1899	Falcon condensers
7	Thos. Green & Sons Ltd	HP cyl. 9" dia.14" stroke LP cyl. 14" dia.14" stroke	5/1890	1899	Falcon
8	Thos. Green & Sons Ltd	HP cyl. 9" dia.14" stroke LP cyl. 14" dia.14" stroke	3/1891	1899	Burrell condenser
9	Thos. Green & Sons Ltd	HP cyl. 9" dia.14" stroke LP cyl. 14" dia.14" stroke	11/1891	1899	Burrell condenser

Green's works Nos. 1-6: 137-141; 7: 144; 8: 158; 9: 168   **LIVERY**: Red with gold lining

TRAILER CARS

Fleet No.	Manufacturer	Type	Seating	Date in Service	Date Withdrawn	Remarks
1-10	G.F.Milnes & Co.	8-wheel 28'6" long	H36/28	1890-3	1899	7' wide; 14'2" high

2 cars delivered 1/1890 & at least 6 more by 7/1890. 8-9: 1891?, 10: 1893?.
Seating capacity controversial. Some sources say 68 in total.   **LIVERY**: Unknown.

ELECTRIC CARS

LANCASHIRE LIGHT RAILWAYS CO. LTD.

Fleet No.	Manufacturer	Type	Seating	Date in Service	Date W/drawn	Remarks
37-41	G.F.Milnes & Co.	4 wheel; 3-window; canopied Busch 6' trucks; 2 x 25hp Witting-Eborell motors	O35/22	1902	1919	To SLT
42-43*	British Electric Car Co.	4-wheel; 4-window; short canopies	O33/22	1902	1919	To SLT
44-46	Cars on loan from SLT identical to 37-41.					

* Believed to have been cancelled order by Aberdeen Corporation.

NEW ST. HELENS & DISTRICT TRAMWAYS CO. LTD.

Fleet No.	Manufacturer	Type	Seating	Date in Service	Date W/drawn	Remarks
1-15 (odd Nos.)	Brush 4-wheel	Brill 21E 6' trucks 2 x BTH GE52-6T 20 hp motors	O29/24	1899	1919	To St.H CT
2-16 (even Nos.)	Brush 8-wheel	Brill 22E bogies 2 x BTH GE52-6T 20 hp motors	O37/36	1899	1919	To St H CT
17-36	Brush 8-wheel	Brill 22E bogies 2 x Westinghouse No. 38 motors	O43/36	1899-1900	1919	To St.H CT
	(Four of these cars withdrawn during 1914-18 war; others renumbered as necessary to 17-32)					
33-36	English Electric	bogie 5-window equipment unknown	O 74?	1918	1919	To St H CT

17-36 had Mozley reversed stairs.   **LIVERY**: 1899-c.1913 – Dark red and white   1913-19 – Green and white

ST. HELENS CORPORATION TRAMWAYS

Cars 1-36 of New St. Helens & District Tramways Co. were transferred to the Corporation and retained their numbers for the time being. Subsequent alterations as follows:-

1-15 (odd numbers)

1, 7, 11	rebuilt as fully enclosed low-height car with 10' radial truck in 1925-26 Seats 46/29; 7 mounted on bogies and renumbered 15 in March 1929
3, 15	rebuilt as above but with open balconies. 15 renumbered 9 in March 1929
5	rebuilt as single deck 36-seat one-man car in 1923
9, 13	remained unrebuilt. 9 renumbered 29 in March 1929

2-16 (even numbers)

2, 4, 6, 8, 10	rebuilt with top-covers and open balconies
12, 16	probably as 2 etc. but not certain. Exchanged numbers with each other in March 1929
14	Rebuilt as top covered low-height car with 10ft radial truck; renumbered 7 in March 1929
17-32	remained unrebuilt; 24 converted to works car 1923; unnumbered from 1929. Renumberings March 1929: 17-18 to 30-31; 20-21 to 32-33; 22 to 34; 26-27 to 35-36; 29 to 37; 32 to 38
33-36	top-covered 1920. Renumbered 17-20 in March 1929.

ADDITIONAL CARS

Fleet No.	Manufacturer	Type	Seating	Date in Service	Date W/drawn	Remarks
37-44	Brush 4-wheel	Brush 21E 7'6" trucks	H50	1921	1935-36	
		2 x BTH GE200K 40hp motors;				open balconies
		All vestibuled; 42 rebuilt as fully enclosed; renumbered 21-28 March 1929				
30-31	Dick Kerr 8-wheel	Burnley bogies	S54	1927	1935	
		2 x Westinghouse 200				
		30-35 hp motors				
		ex-Wigan Corporation. 68, 77 (not necessarily in order). New 1904. Renumbered 13-14 March 1929				
		In addition, there was an unnumbered rail grinder, scrapped 1931.				

WITHDRAWALS (New numbers in parenthesis).

1927:	19, 30-31
1929:	5, 13, 23, 25, 28
1930:	27 (36), 29 (37)
1931:	17 (30), 18 (31), 20 (32), 21 (33), 22 (34), 24 (works car), 26 (35), 32 (38).
1932:	9 (29), 12 (16)
1934:	2, 4, 8, 16 (12), 33-36 (17-20)
1935:	1, 3, 6, 7 (15), 10, 11, 14 (7), 15 (9) 30-31 (13-14), 38 (22)
1936:	37 (21), 39-44 (23-28)

TROLLEYBUS FLEET 1927-56

Fleet No. 1	2	3	Reg. No.	Chassis Make and Type	Body Make	Type & Capacity	Year in Service	Year Withdrawn	Notes
1-4	101-4	161/3/4	DJ 3243-6	Garrett 0	Ransomes	B35C	1927	1936-8	
5	100	110	DJ 3684	Ransomes 2-axle	Ransomes	B32C	1928	1938	
105-8			DJ 4081-4	Ransomes 2-axle	Ransomes	B35C	1929	1938-9	
109			ET 5968	Ransomes 2-axle	Ransomes	B35C	1929	1940	
110	115		DJ 4845	Ransomes D6 3-axle	Ransomes	L32/28R	1931	1942	
111-4			DJ 4846-9	Ransomes D6 3-axle	Ransomes	L32/28R	1931	1942	
116-20			DJ 6051-5	Ransomes D4 2-axle	Brush	L24/26R	1934	1945-50	119 rebod.E.Lancs /43
121			DJ 6106	Leyland TBD2	Brush	L24/26R	1934	1952	Rebod.E.Lancs /46
122-5			DJ 6120-3	Leyland TBD2	Brush	L24/26R	1934	1952	Rebod.E.Lancs 45-7
126-36			DJ 6453-63	Leyland TBD2	Massey	L24/26R	1935	1952	Rebod.E.Lancs 45-6
137-41			DJ 6863-7	Ransomes D4 2-axle	Massey	L24/26R	1936	1949-52	
142-4			DJ 7236-8	Ransomes D4 2 axle	Massey	L24/26R	1936-7	1949-50	
101-4	301-4		DJ 7428-31	Leyland TBD2	Massey	L24/26R	1937	1956	Rebod.E.Lancs 47-8
145-56			DJ 8120-31	Ransomes D4 2-axle	Massey	L24/26R	1938	1950-52	
157-66		357-66	DJ 9005-14	Sunbeam MF2 8ft	Massey	L24/26R	1942	1955-56	
105-14		305-14	DJ 9183-92	Sunbeam W	Roe	L24/26R	1945	1956-58	
174-81		374-81	BDJ 74-81	Sunbeam F4	East Lancs.	H29/26R	1951	1958	
182-9	382-9		BDJ 82-9	BUT 9611T	East Lancs.	H30/26R	1951	1958	

BODY REFURBISHMENT PROGRAMME 1947-49

Air Despatch/Bruce Coachworks Ltd., Cardiff:-   145, 156, 157, 158, 161, 162, 163
Bankfield Engineering Ltd., Southport:-   137, 138, 141, 146, 147, 151, 152
East Lancashire Coachbuilders Ltd.:-   165
Marsden (Coachbuilders) Ltd., Warrington:-   148, 149, 150*, 154, 155
Massey Bros. Ltd.:-   160*, 166
Corporation Transport workshop:-   159, 164

* including accident damage.

ST. HELENS CORPORATION TRANSPORT

MOTOR BUS FLEET
1923-74

Fleet No. 1	2	3	Reg. No.	Chassis Make and Type	Body Make	Type & Capacity	Year in Service	Year W/drawn	Notes
1	50		DJ 1871	Bristol 2-t.	Bristol	B24F	1924	1933	
2	51	58	DJ 1810	Guy BA	Guy	B20F	1923	1934	
3	52		DJ 1830	Guy BA	Guy	B20F	1923	1934	
4	53	56	DJ 2036	Guy BA	Guy	B20F	1924	1934	Rebodied St.Helens Corp. B20F 5/30
5	54		DJ 2063	Guy BB	Strachan & Brown	B32R	1924	1933	To B29R 11/32
6	55		DJ 2289	Guy BB	Guy	B32F	1925	1933	
7	56		DJ 2575	Guy BB	Guy	B32F	1925	1933	To B30D 11/32
8	57		DJ 2784	Guy BB	Guy	B32F	1926	1934	Rebodied St.Helens Corp. B32F 8/31, B30F 11/32
9	58		DJ 2821	Guy BB	Guy	B20F	1926	1933	Rebodied St.Helens Corp. B32F 8/29, B30F 11/32

Vehicles acquired from St. Helens & District Motor Service Co. Ltd. 1.6.27

Fleet No. 1	2	3	Reg. No.	Chassis Make and Type	Body Make	Type & Capacity	Year in Service	Year W/drawn	Notes
10	67		DJ 539	Daimler Y	Massey	B30F	1921	1931	to B28F 1/29
11	69		DJ 384	Daimler B	Massey	B26R	1914	1929	
12	68		DJ 1437	Daimler CK	NCME	B28R	1921	1934	Body ex 69(11) 2/31. to B24R 11/32
13	59		DJ 575	Daimler Y	Hora?	B28F	1921	1931	Rebodied St.Helens Corp. B26F 10/27
14	60		B 8841	Leyland N (?)	Hora	B32R	1919	1931	
15	61	58	DJ 2372	Leyland C7	NCME	B32F	1925	1934	Reseated B26F 12/32
16	62	59	DJ 2579	Leyland C7	Leyland	B30F	1926	1934	Reseated B28F 11/32; diesel engine fitted 1/33
17	20		DJ 411	Garner	?	B20F	1921	1928	

Fleet No. 1	2	3	Reg. No.	Chassis Make and Type	Body Make	Type & Capacity	Year in Service	Year W/drawn	Notes
17-18	63-4	83-4	DJ 3648-9	Bristol B	Bristol	B32F	1928	1937	
19-20	65-6	85-6	DJ 3650-1	Leyland PLSC3	Ransomes	B32F	1928	1938	
69-70	89-90		DJ 4834-5	Leyland TD1	Leyland	L24/24R	1931	1940	
71-72	91-2		DJ 5042-3	Leyland TD1	Leyland	L24/24R	1931	1948	
59-60	73-4		DJ 5405-6	Crossley Condor	Crossley	L24/24R	1932	1947	
67	75		DJ 5407	Crossley Condor	Crossley	L24/24R	1932	1941	
76-78			DJ 5684-6	Leyland TD2	Leyland	L24/24R	1933	1947	
73-4	60-1		EK 4994/6	Bristol B	NCME	B32F	1933	1935	Ex Wigan Corp.21/23 1/33. New 1927.
75	62	82	EK 6001	Bristol B	NCME	B32F	1933	1937	Ex Wigan Corp.30 1/33. New 1927
51-5	*		DJ 6056/9/8/	Leyland TS6C	Eng. Elec.	B32F	1934	1950-4	* Renumbered 255/8/7/9/6 60/57/48. 256-7 rebod. Roe B36R & to TS6 6/49
56-8	*		DJ 6336/8/7	Leyland TS6C	Eng. Elec.	B32F	1935	1950-4	* Renumbered 260/2/1 3/48. 260 (56) rebodied B36R and to TS6 6/49
59	90	51	DJ 6339	Leyland TS6C	Eng. Elec.	B32F	1935	1956	Rebod. East Lancs L27/26R and to TD3 7/46
60-1	251-2		DJ 6578-9	Leyland TS6C	Leyland	B32F	1935	1952-4	251 rebodied Roe B33D 8/50
67-8	253-4		DJ 6580-1	Leyland TS6C	Leyland	B32F	1935	1953	Rebod. Roe B33D 8/50
62-6	240-4		DJ 7591-5	Leyland TS8C	Leyland	B32F	1937	1951-2	
79	245		DJ 7596	Leyland TS8C	Leyland	B32F	1937	1950	
80-4	246-50		DJ 8090-4	Leyland TS8C	Leyland	B32F	1938	1951-2	

Fleet No. 1	2	3	Reg. No.	Chassis Make and Type	Body Make	Type & Capacity	Year in Service	Year W/drawn	Notes
85	54		DJ 8074	Leyland TD5C	Leyland	L24/26R	1938	1955	
86-8			DJ 8075-7	Leyland TD5C	Leyland	L24/26R	1938	1953-4	
69-72	81-4		DJ 8675-8	Leyland TD7C	Leyland	L24/26R	1939	1953-6	71 rebuilt by E.Lancs after fire as L27/26R 12/45; 81 reno'd 83 2/54, A52 8/54
89	A89	A53	DJ 8973	Leyland TD7	Leyland	L27/26R	1942	1955	'Unfrozen'.Built for SMT
93-6	A93-6		DJ 9048-51	Guy Arab I 5LW	NCME	L24/26R	1942	1955-6	
97	A97		DJ 9089	Guy Arab I 5LW	NCME	L24/26R	1943	1956	
98			DJ 9076	Guy Arab II 5LW	NCME	L27/26R	1943	1950	
99-100	A99/B100		DJ 9099/100	Guy Arab II 5LW	NCME	L27/26R	1943	1954-6	99 to L24/26 47 or 48
75	91	A98	DJ 9162	Guy Arab II 5LW	Weymann	L27/28R	1945	1956	
90	92		DJ 9163	Guy Arab II 5LW	Weymann	L27/28R	1945	1956	
49-50	B49-50		DJ 9267-8	Bristol K6A	Strachans	L27/28R	1946	1957	
47-48			DJ 9269-70	Bristol K6A	Strachans	L27/28R	1946	1957	
17-18			EK 8103/7	Leyland TD1	NCME	L24/24R	1946	1950	Ex Wigan 63A/67A
19			EK 7910	Leyland TD1	Leyland	L24/24R	1946	1950	Ex Wigan 42 New 1931
20			EK 9320	Leyland TD2	NCME	L24/24R	1946	1949	Ex Wigan 35 New 1933
44-6	B44-6		DJ 9837-9	Bristol K6A	East Lancs	L27/26R	1947	1959	
41-3	B41-3		DJ 9917-9	Leyland PD1	East Lancs.	L27/26R	1947	1960	
40-35	B40-35		ADJ 187-92	AEC Regent II	East Lancs.	L27/26R	1948	1957-8	
201-4			ADJ 193-6	Bristol L6A	Roe	B35R	1948	1955/63	
205-8			ADJ 324-7	Bristol L6A	Roe	B35R	1948	1956/64	
27-34	C27-34		ADJ 835/28-34	AEC Regent III	East Lancs.	L27/26R	1949	1958-9	
59-73	D59-73		BDJ 59-73	AEC Regent III	Park Royal	H30/26R	1950	1962	RT
209			BDJ 329	AEC Regal IV	Roe	B42D	1951	1965	
1-25	D1-25		BDJ 801-25	AEC Regent III	Park Royal	H30/26R	1951-2	1960-2	RT D11-2 reno'd D31-2 10/61
E74-77			CDJ 719-22	Leyland PD2/9	Davies	H30/26R	1954	1965	
E78-82			CDJ 878-82	Leyland PD2/9	Davies	H30/26R	1954	1964-5	
E83-86			DDJ 490-3	Leyland PD2/22	East Lancs.	H30/28R	1954	1967-8	
E87-91			DDJ 525-9	Leyland PD2/22	East Lancs.	H30/28R	1954	1967-8	
F101-9			EDJ 501-9	Leyland PD2/20	East Lancs.	H33/28R	1955	1968	
F110-1			EDJ 510-1	Leyland PD2/20	Weymann	H33/28R	1957	1967	
F112			EDJ 512	Leyland PD2/20	Davies	H33/28R	1956	1968	
F113-7			EDJ 513-7	Leyland PD2/20	Weymann	H33/28R	1957	1968	
G118-27			FDJ 818-27	Leyland PD2/20	East Lancs.	H33/28R	1956-7	1966-9	
G128-33			FDJ 828-33	Leyland PD2/20	Weymann	H33/28R	1956	1969	
H134-39			GDJ 434-9	AEC Regent V	Weymann	H33/28R	1957	1973-4	
J140-55			HDJ 740-55	AEC Regent V	Weymann	H33/28R	1958	1969-77	
J156-63			HDJ 756-63	AEC Regent V	East Lancs.	H33/28R	1958	1968-71	
K164-71			KDJ 364-71	AEC Regent V	Weymann	H36/28R	1959	1970-1	
K199			KDJ 999	AEC Regent V	East Lancs.	H41/32F	1959	1971	
K172-5			LDJ 982-5	Leyland PD2/30	Weymann	H36/28R	1960	1972	
K176-9			LDJ 986-9	Leyland PD2/30	East Lancs.	H36/28R	1960	1972	
L1-7			ODJ 941-7	AEC Regent V	MCCW	H36/28R	1961	1972/77	
L8-12			PDJ 708-12	Leyland PD2A/30	East Lancs.	H36/28R	1961	1973/76	
L13-19			PDJ 813-9	Leyland PD2A/30	MCCW	H36/28R	1962	1977-8	
L20-25			RDJ 100-5	Leyland PD2A/30	MCCW	H36/28R	1962	1976/79	
L26-32			RDJ 726-32	Leyland PD2A/30	East Lancs.	H36/28R	1962	1973-8	
200			SDJ 162	Leyland L2	Duple	C41C	1962	1971	
L33-40			SDJ 353-60	AEC Regent V	MCCW	H36/28R	1962	1977/79	
210-2			TDJ 610-2	AEC Reliance	Marshall	B45F	1963	1973	
213-4			DDJ 213-4C	AEC Reliance	Marshall	B45F	1965	1977	To B41D 11/66
L41-45			FDJ 341-5C	Leyland PD2A/30	East Lancs.	H36/28R	1965	1976-7	
L46-49			FDJ 346-9C	Leyland PD2A/30	MCCW	H36/28R	1965	1977-8	
50-55			MDJ 550-5E	Leyland PD2A/27	East Lancs.	H37/28R	1967	1979-80	
56-58			MDJ 916-8E	AEC Regent V	MCCW	H37/28R	1967	1980-82	
215-23			RDJ 215-23F	AEC Swift	Marshall	B44D	1968	1981	
224-32			TDJ 224-32F	AEC Swift	Marshall	B44D	1968	1981	
233-41			XDJ 233-41H	AEC Swift	Marshall	B44D	1969	1982-3	
242-59			EDJ 242-59J	AEC Swift	Marshall	B44D	1971	1983-4	
201			KKU 77F	Bedford VAM70	Duple	C45F	1971	1981	ex N.Boyes New 1968
260-8			JDJ 260-8K	AEC Swift	Marshall	B44D	1972	1984-6	
269-77			PDJ 269-77L	AEC Swift	Marshall	B42D	1973	1984-6	
291-3			NTC 108-10G	AEC Swift	Alexander	B43D	1973	1981	ex-LUT new 1969
131/4			LFY 31/4	Leyland PD2/20	Weymann	H32/28R	1974	1975	ex-Southport new 1956
137			MWM 37	Leyland PD2/20	Weymann	H32/28R	1974	1974	ex Southport new 1957

VEHICLES ORDERED BY ST. HELENS CORPORATION BUT DELIVERED TO MERSEYSIDE PTE.

278-86	GEM 598-606N	AEC Swift	Marshall	B42D	1975	1984-6	

VEHICLES ON HIRE

	HT 4018	Bristol 4-ton	Bristol	B30R	1921	1921	Bristol T&C Co.
	HT 4367	Bristol 4-ton	Bristol	B32R	1921	1922	Bristol T&C Co.
	KB 1968-9	AEC YC	Hora	B32R	1921	1921	Liverpool Corp
	KB 1985	AEC YC	Hora	B32R	1921	1921	Liverpool Corp
31/7	WH 7807/13	Leyland TD4C	Massey	H26/26R	1941	1944	Bolton Corp.31/7
23-21	DB 5132/4/ 5216	TSM B10A	Mumford	C32R	1946	1947	W.National 41/3,17
24	ET 4919	Bristol B	Roe	B32C	1946	1947	Rotherham Corp 166
25-26	VV 1164-5	Dennis Lancet	Grose	B26F	1946	1948	Northampton Corp 55/6
14-15	EN 4312-3	Leyland LT1	Roe	B31D	1947	1948	Bury Corp 14-5
27-28	TF 6362-3	Leyland LT3	Massey	B32D	1947	1948	Leigh Corp 43-4
—	PTO 708G	AEC Swift	NCME	B43D	1974	1974	Nottingham Corp 708
—	YFY 2M	Leyland National 1151/2R		B46D	1974	1974	Southport Corp. 2

Various demonstrators were also on hire from time to time.

BODY REFURBISHMENT PROGRAMME 1947-50

Bankfield Engineering Ltd., Southport:- 17, 19, 64 (242), 69, 72, 85, 86*
Bruce Coachworks Ltd., Cardiff:- 96, 97.
James Hilton & Sons Ltd., Leigh:- 51 (255), 52, 57*, 68 (254), 70, 87
Lyon & Pye, St.Helens:- 61 (252)
Marsden (Coachbuilders) Ltd., Warrington 18
Corporation Transport Workshops 100
      * including accident damage.

ST. HELENS CORPORATION TRANSPORT OPERATING STATISTICS

Year Ending 31st March	Revenue £000s	Per Vehicle mile (p)	Passengers 000s	Mileage 000s	Gross Expenses £000s	Net Surplus (Deficit) £000s
1920	43	8.83	5523	485	46	(3)
1921	110	10.95	11037	1003	114	(4)
1922	93	10.99	8601	841	82	10
1923	82	8.68	8386	947	73	9
1924	76	7.82	8858	991	73	4
1925	85	7.74	9740	1102	80	5
1926	90	7.85	10424	1150	82	8
1927	84	7.24	9603	1164	84	1
1928	99	6.93	11468	1424	90	9
1929	99	6.62	11343	1495	92	7
1930	105	6.55	12364	1608	96	9
1931	109	6.30	13096	1735	100	9
1932	107	5.65	13014	1883	102	5
1933	104	5.27	12515	1968	101	3
1934	107	5.13	12804	2080	97	9
1935	116	5.24	13920	2207	108	8
1936	128	5.13	16111	2490	118	10
1937	138	5.01	18408	2753	138	-
1938	152	5.24	20449	2900	134	18
1939	168	5.15	22951	3256	147	20
1940	172	5.42	25190	3181	156	16
1941	209	6.94	27656	3009	175	34
1942	277	8.55	35356	3251	200	77
1943	303	9.07	38435	3344	224	79
1944	321	9.45	40660	3392	240	81
1945	345	9.91	42872	3464	255	89
1946	334	9.15	41848	3637	262	72
1947	397	8.51	48872	4664	336	61
1948	432	8.34	52506	5094	397	35
1949	462	8.50	55157	5441	443	19
1950	471	8.38	55559	5623	474	(3)
1951	468	8.52	55199	5496	481	(12)
1952	521	9.53	55158	5470	539	(17)
1953	598	10.24	55431	5845	597	1
1954	639	10.95	57163	5835	611	28
1955	662	10.81	58800	6121	637	25
1956	686	11.00	60343	6233	675	11
1957	760	12.31	59213	6171	719	40
1958	772	12.38	57809	6237	765	8
1959	803	13.00	56726	6175	748	54
1960	794	13.21	56117	6015	732	62
1961	793	13.41	55255	5910	758	35
1962	800	13.54	54940	5907	813	(14)
1963	843	14.14	52636	5963	853	(10)
1964	896	14.88	52040	6024	912	(15)
1965	895	14.92	50777	5996	962	(68)
1966	968	16.27	47372	5947	1040	(72)
1967	1106	19.15	43231	5776	1074	32
1968	1047	19.37	39236	5407	1057	(10)
1969	982	20.73	34602	4738	1019	(37)
1970	1034	23.45	32456	4409	1023	22
1971	1066	25.33	31371	4227	1100	(33)
1972	1227	27.99	30680	4383	1181	45
1973	1247	28.18	30999	4425	1293	(46)

CHAIRMEN OF THE TRANSPORT COMMITTEE

1919-45	Alderman W. Rudd
1945-61	Alderman W. Marshall
1961-71	Counc. W.L. Williams
1972-74	Counc. J. Mulcrow

GENERAL MANAGERS

St. Helens experienced many changes of manager; there is no suggestion that it was a bad employer but the varied experience which the undertaking gave, and the satisfactory financial results, fitted managers for appointments in larger undertakings elsewhere.

ST. HELENS & DISTRICT TRAMWAYS CO. LTD

1890-91	A. Johnson
1891-8	I.F. Cuttler

NEW ST. HELENS & DISTRICT TRAMWAYS CO. LTD?

1898-1901	I.F. Cuttler
1901-5	Walter Vaux
1905-6	W. Hutchings
1906-10	J.R. Salter (also general manager of SLT Co.)
1910-19	C.D. Stanley

ST. HELENS CORPORATION

1919-24	L.C.F. Bellamy
1924	F.H. Glover
1925	W. Vane Morland
1925-28	D.E. Bell
1928-33	Ben England
1933-39	A.A. Jackson
1939-40	G.H. Pulfrey
1941-45	W.M. Little
1945-49	G.W. Robb
1949-52	R. Edgeley Cox
1952-61	J.C. Wake
1961-73	A.C. Barlow
1973-74	L.H. Newall (acting)

Preserved St. Helens Corporation Transport Vehicles

The following passenger vehicles are still in existence and the table below gives their location:-

Tram – The body of St. Helens single-deck tram numbered 14 ex-Wigan Corporation. Number 72 has survived as a pavilion for St. Helens Parish Church Bowling Club on the site of the St. Helens Parish Church bowling green where it is used to stock items used by the bowlers and to act as a shelter in wet weather.

Trolleybus – 387 BUT 9611T with East Lancs. body BDJ 87. Fully restored in its St. Helens condition except for the seat, this trolleybus is preserved at the Sandtoft Trolleybus Museum.

Motor buses – A considerable number of buses are preserved as follows:-

Fleet No.	Reg. No.	Chassis	Body	Location
67	BDJ 67	AEC RT	Park Royal	St. Helens Transport Museum
78	CDJ 878	Leyland PD2	Davies	St. Helens Transport Museum
135	GDJ 435	AEC Regent V	Weymann	St. Helens Transport Museum
153	HDJ 753	AEC Regent V	Weymann	St. Helens Transport Museum
199	KDJ 999	AEC Regent V	East Lancs	St. Helens Transport Museum
175	LDJ 985	Leyland PD2	Weymann	St. Helens Transport Museum
212	TDJ 612	AEC Reliance	Marshall	St. Helens Transport Museum
54	MDJ 554E	Leyland PD2	East Lancs.	St. Helens Transport Museum
55	MDJ 555E	Leyland PD2	East Lancs.	St. Helens Transport Museum
58	MDJ 918E	AEC Regent V	MCCW	Mersey & Calder Preservation Group
244	EDJ 244J	AEC Swift	Marshall	Mersey & Calder Preservation Group
260	JDJ 260K	AEC Swift	Marshall	St. Helens Transport Museum
269	PDJ 269L	AEC Swift	Marshall	St. Helens Transport Museum

In addition to the above AEC RT BDJ 808 has survived as a training vehicle with the top deck of its Park body removed and the rear platform removed. It is located in the St. Helens Transport Museum.

Joint author Mervyn Ashton has a half share in this St. Helens trolleybus at the Sandtoft Trolleybus Museum seen here together with a couple of Walsall examples.

PHOTOCREDITS

A worthy candidate for preservation would have been this Roe-bodied Bristol which ended its days as a mobile shop. Sadly, as in so many cases, the preservation movement had not got under way in time for such a gem to be preserved.

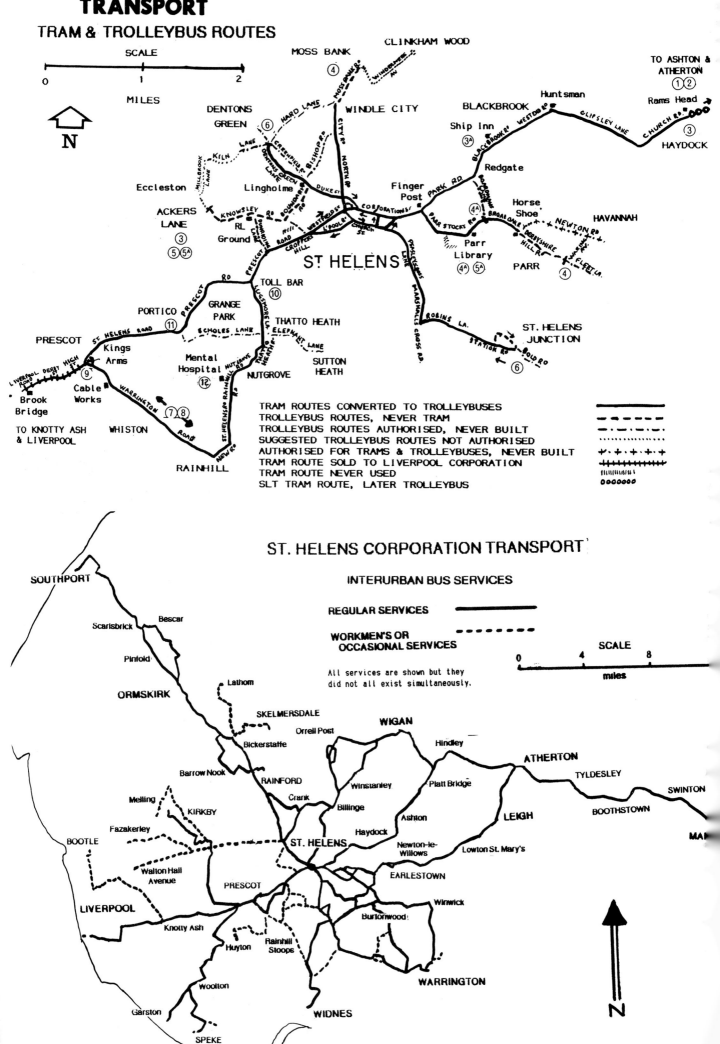

ST HELENS CORPORATION TRANSPORT

TRAM & TROLLEYBUS ROUTES

SCALE

0   1   2

MILES

N

TRAM ROUTES CONVERTED TO TROLLEYBUSES
TROLLEYBUS ROUTES, NEVER TRAM
TROLLEYBUS ROUTES AUTHORISED, NEVER BUILT
SUGGESTED TROLLEYBUS ROUTES NOT AUTHORISED
AUTHORISED FOR TRAMS & TROLLEYBUSES, NEVER BUILT
TRAM ROUTE SOLD TO LIVERPOOL CORPORATION
TRAM ROUTE NEVER USED
SLT TRAM ROUTE, LATER TROLLEYBUS

ST. HELENS CORPORATION TRANSPORT

INTERURBAN BUS SERVICES

REGULAR SERVICES

WORKMEN'S OR OCCASIONAL SERVICES

All services are shown but they
did not all exist simultaneously.

SCALE

0   4   8

miles

N

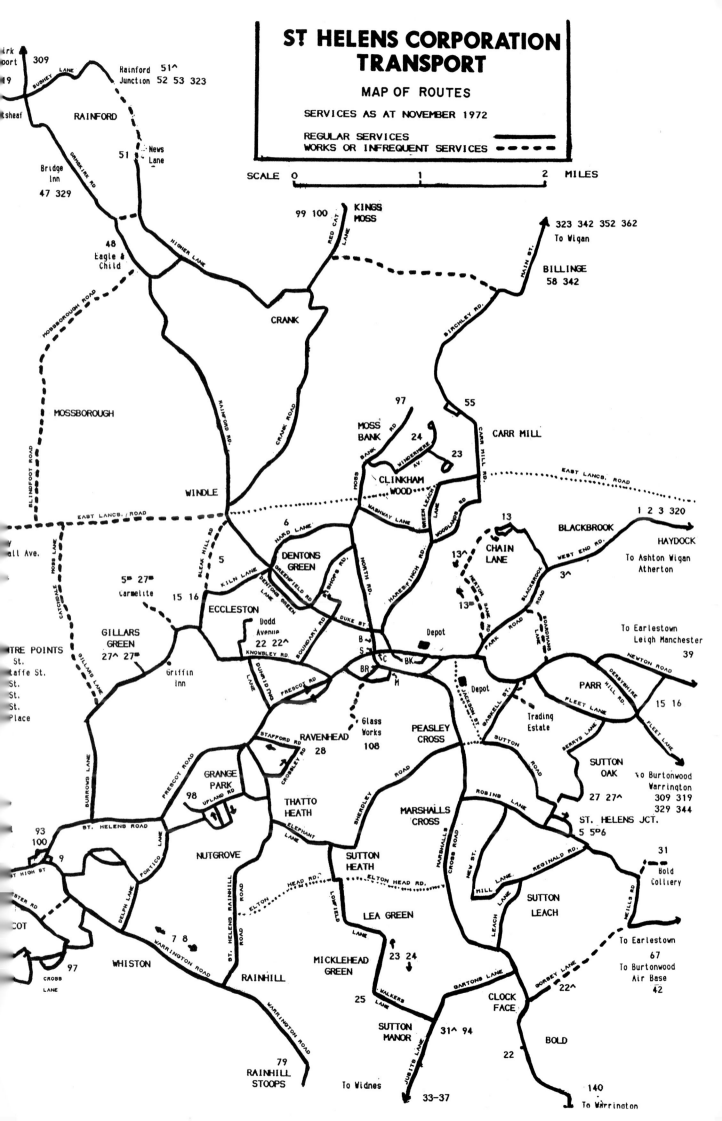

ST HELENS CORPORATION TRANSPORT

MAP OF ROUTES

SERVICES AS AT NOVEMBER 1972

| REGULAR SERVICES | ———— |
| WORKS OR INFREQUENT SERVICES | – – – – |

SCALE 0   1   2 MILES